# Easter Rising 1916

Birth of the Irish Republic

Campaign • 180

# Easter Rising 1916

Birth of the Irish Republic

Michael McNally • Illustrated by Peter Dennis

First published in Great Britain in 2007 by Osprey Publishing,
Midland House, West Way, Botley, Oxford OX2 0PH, UK
44-02 23rd St, Suite 219, Long Island City, NY 11101, USA
E-mail: info@ospreypublishing.com

A CIP catalogue record for this book is available from the British Library

ISBN 978 1 84603 067 3

Page layout by: The Black Spot
Index by Alison Worthington
Typeset in Helvetica Neue and ITC New Baskerville
Maps by The Map Studio Ltd
3D bird's-eye views by The Black Spot
Originated by United Graphic Ltd, Singapore
Printed in China through Worldprint

09 10 11 12 13    12 11 10 9 8 7 6 5 4 3

FOR A CATALOGUE OF ALL BOOKS PUBLISHED BY OSPREY MILITARY
AND AVIATION PLEASE CONTACT:

Osprey Direct, c/o Random House Distribution Center,
400 Hahn Road, Westminster, MD 21157
Email: uscustomerservice@ospreypublishing.com

Osprey Direct, The Book Service Ltd, Distribution Centre,
Colchester Road, Frating Green, Colchester, Essex, CO7 7DW
E-mail: customerservice@ospreypublishing.com

**www.ospreypublishing.com**

Front cover: Henry Street in the aftermath of the Rising, with the Nelson Pillar
in the background. (Courtesy of the National Library of Ireland, Keogh 114)

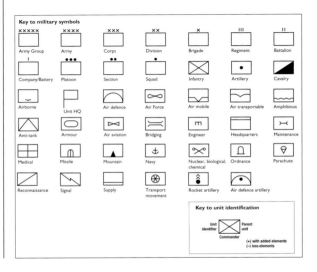

Key to military symbols

Key to unit identification

## Author's note

I'd like to dedicate this book to the memory of my father-
in-law, Bernhard Lagemann, who sadly died during its
preparation, and to my youngest son, Liam, who was
born a few days after his grandfather passed away.

I'd also like to thank my wife, Petra, and our eldest
children, Stephen and Elena, for their patience over the
last year, and to the following who have given help and
advice with the project: Jon Casey, Andy Copestake, Rob
Anderson, David Murphy, Seán O'Brógaín, Ian Spence,
Glenn Thompson, Jay Currah of the Enfield Rifles website,
Bruce Gudmundsson, Dr John Bourne of the University of
Birmingham; Lár Joye, Róisín Miles, Brenda Malone, Aoife
McBride and Finbarr Connolly all of the National Museum
of Ireland, Dublin; Sara Smyth of the National Library
of Ireland, Dublin; to An Post, Dublin, for granting me
permission to have access to the GPO plans; to Valerie
Ingram, Nuala Canny and the staff of the OPW library,
Dublin, and to the various photographic libraries who have
graciously provided illustrations to accompany the text.

Finally a heartfelt thank you to my editor, Marcus
Cowper, for his support during a difficult year and to Peter
Dennis, for his patience and for producing some truly
evocative artwork to accompany my text.

## Artist's note

## Imperial War Museum Collections

Many of the photos in this book come from the Imperial
War Museum's huge collections which cover all aspects
of conflict involving Britain and the Commonwealth since
the start of the twentieth century. These rich resources
are available online to search, browse and buy at
www.iwmcollections.org.uk. In addition to Collections
Online, you can visit the Visitor Rooms where you can
explore over 8 million photographs, thousands of hours
of moving images, the largest sound archive of its kind
in the world, thousands of diaries and letters written
by people in wartime, and a huge reference library. To
make an appointment, call (020) 7416 5320, or e-mail
mail@iwm.org.uk. Imperial War Museum www.iwm.org.uk

# CONTENTS

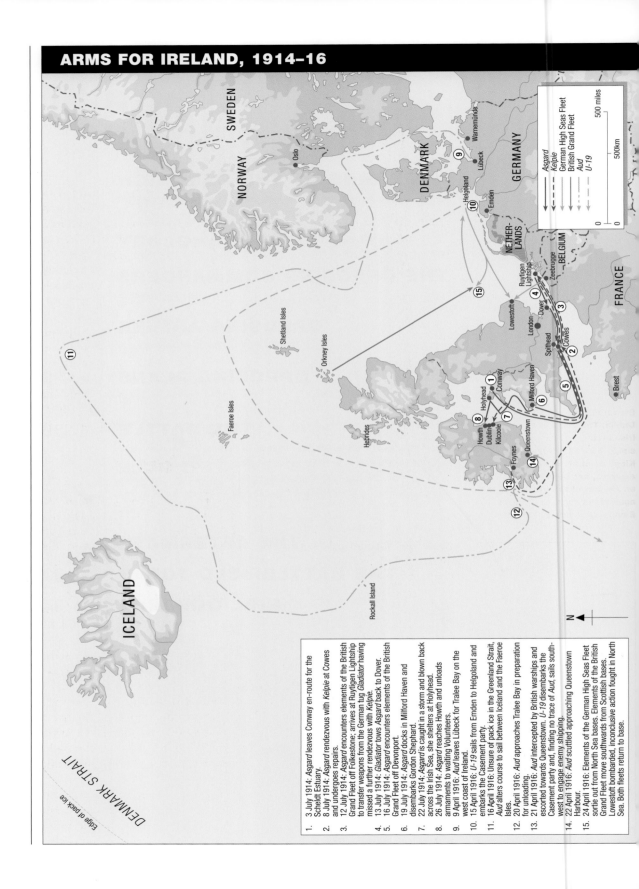

# ARMS FOR IRELAND, 1914–16

Legend:
- Asgard
- Kelpie
- German High Seas Fleet
- British Grand Fleet
- Aud
- U-19

0   500 miles
0   500km

1. 3 July 1914: *Asgard* leaves Conway en-route for the Scheldt Estuary.
2. 8 July 1914: *Asgard* rendezvous with *Kelpie* at Cowes and undergoes repairs.
3. 12 July 1914: *Asgard* encounters elements of the British Grand Fleet off Folkestone; arrives at Ruytigen Lightship to transfer weapons from the German tug *Gladiator* having missed a further rendezvous with *Kelpie*.
4. 13 July 1914: *Gladiator* tows *Asgard* back to Dover.
5. 16 July 1914: *Asgard* encounters elements of the British Grand Fleet off Devonport.
6. 19 July 1914: *Asgard* docks in Milford Haven and disembarks Gordon Shephard.
7. 22 July 1914: *Asgard* is caught in a storm and blown back across the Irish Sea, she shelters at Holyhead.
8. 26 July 1914: *Asgard* reaches Howth and unloads armaments to waiting Volunteers.
9. 9 April 1916: *Aud* leaves Lübeck for Tralee Bay on the west coast of Ireland.
10. 15 April 1916: *U-19* sails from Emden to Helgoland and embarks the Casement party.
11. 16 April 1916: Unsure of pack ice in the Greenland Strait, *Aud* alters course to sail between Iceland and the Faeroe Isles.
12. 20 April 1916: *Aud* approaches Tralee Bay in preparation for unloading.
13. 21 April 1916: *Aud* intercepted by British warships and escorted towards Queenstown. *U-19* disembarks the Casement party and, finding no trace of *Aud*, sails south-west to engage enemy shipping.
14. 22 April 1916: *Aud* scuttled approaching Queenstown Harbour.
15. 24 April 1916: Elements of the German High Seas Fleet sortie out from North Sea bases. Elements of the British Grand Fleet move southwards from Scottish bases. Lowestoft bombarded, inconclusive action fought in North Sea. Both fleets return to base.

# ORIGINS OF THE CAMPAIGN

**D**uring the night of 15 April 1916 the *U-19*, a German submarine under the command of Kapitänleutnant Raimund Weissbach, surfaced off the west coast of Ireland. Although newly promoted, Weissbach was not unfamiliar with Irish waters – In May 1915 he was torpedo officer aboard the *U-20* when she sank the passenger ship *Lusitania* off the Old Head of Kinsale. His mission this time was less warlike and, under the cover of darkness, three Irishmen clambered into the submarine's dinghy and began to make for shore. The first two, Robert Monteith and Daniel Bailey, were members of the 'Irish Brigade', a formation recruited from former British prisoners of war who were willing to fight for Irish independence. The third member of the group was Sir Roger Casement, a Dublin-born former British diplomat who had spent the previous year trying to persuade the German High Command to support and endorse an Irish rebellion but who, disillusioned by what he saw as a complete lack of support from Berlin, was now travelling to Ireland to forestall the proposed uprising.

## THE QUESTION OF HOME RULE

In 1800, the British Government tightened its control over Irish affairs by transferring the Dublin Parliament to London, with Irish MPs forming a parliamentary minority at a time when the nation was united in the face of various foreign crises. However by the end of the 19th century this minority had evolved into the Irish Parliamentary Party (IPP) who would support the Government of the day in return for Home Rule – a restored Irish parliament that would decide Irish affairs. It was an effective strategy leading to the passing of the requisite legislation in 1886 and 1893, but the House of Lords, many members of which belonged to the Anglo-Irish aristocracy, vetoed both bills.

In 1910, this contentious subject was resurrected when a series of miscalculations forced the ruling Liberal Party to come to an accommodation with the IPP in order to avoid the formation of a coalition government. Again the price was to be Irish Home Rule but there was always the question of the Lords' opposition and, unwilling to risk a repeat of earlier attempts to introduce the requisite legislation, an Act of Parliament was passed that reduced their veto to the ability to forestall a bill for four years before it could be entered on the statute books and become law.

Theoretically Home Rule was now a certainty, and in April 1912 a bill to this effect was passed in the House of Commons; on paper at least, the efforts of the Irish parliamentarians had been justified. In domestic matters they would see to their own affairs, whilst deferring to

Statue of Cuchulain, GPO, Dublin. The death of the mythical Irish hero Cuchulain, killed whilst single-handedly defending the Kingdom of Ulster against its enemies, has been used here as an allegory of the Irish struggle against the might of the British Empire. (Author's collection)

Westminster in matters of foreign policy, customs duties and defence – the only cloud to darken the horizon was the inevitable delay imposed by the House of Lords.

Other clouds were soon to appear. In June 1914 the Archduke Franz-Ferdinand, heir to the Austrian throne was assassinated at Sarajevo and, with Austria preparing to retaliate against Serbia, Tsar Nicholas II of Russia expressed his sympathy and support for the Serbs whilst the German Kaiser, Wilhelm II, offered his assistance to the Austrians. As the political dominoes began to fall, France entered the dispute on the side of her ally, Russia, and, at midnight on 4 August 1914, following the German invasion of Belgium, Britain declared war on Germany.

An honourable man, and perhaps deluded by the common conviction that the war would be a short-lived affair, and in the belief that Imperial Germany was the common enemy, John Redmond – leader of the IPP – offered to postpone the implementation of Home Rule until the end of hostilities, whilst also urging his supporters to enlist in Britain's armed forces. Many Irish nationalists heeded Redmond's words, but a small but influential group took an opposite view adhering to the old adage that 'England's adversity is Ireland's opportunity'.

## 'ULSTER SHALL FIGHT'

As allies of the Conservative Party, the inevitable Unionist response to increasing nationalist demands for Home Rule was muted by their election victory in 1895, but this parliamentary success was relatively short-lived. The general election of 1906 was a landslide victory for the Liberals, and it was only a series of political miscalculations on the part of the Chancellor, Lloyd George, which forced two elections in 1910 thereby handing the IPP another opportunity to press their suit within the halls of Westminster.

The leader of the Ulster Unionists, the man faced with the task of halting Redmond's resurgent followers, was Sir Edward Carson, a Dublin-

The Parade Ground, Royal Barracks. Now Collins Barracks, the Royal Barracks was garrisoned by the 467 officers and men of the 10th (Service) Battalion, Royal Dublin Fusiliers. (Author's collection)

born barrister. Carson's main fear was that, despite the protestations of previous generations, when push ultimately came to shove Unionists all over the country would baulk at making what he viewed as the necessary sacrifices to defend Ireland's position within a United Kingdom. He need not have worried – in September 1911 a crowd of over 50,000 attended a rally near Belfast to hear him call upon his party to take over the governance of Ulster on the morning that Home Rule became law.

During the early part of 1912 further, larger, rallies were held serving to give notice to the opposition parties that they too could find potential allies in Ireland, and thus a political marriage of convenience was arranged between the Unionists and the Conservative Party in the belief that the question of Home Rule would be the rock upon which the ship of state would founder.

Despite this, and in the wake of several inept attempts by the Government to defuse the situation, Carson still felt that there was a lack of total commitment on the part of the Unionists, and sought to find a device by which a sense of purpose could be instilled in the Party. On Saturday 28 September 1912, he unveiled the terms of Ulster's Solemn League and Covenant and, across the country, 447,197 men and women rushed to sign copies of the document. Further copies were made available for signature in the larger cities in England and Scotland and the number of signatories eventually exceeded 470,000.

Having made his vow to prevent the introduction of Home Rule in Ulster, the next question for Carson was how best to organize his supporters in order to carry out his threat to assume control of the province should it become necessary. For some time Unionists across Ulster had been undergoing military-style training and, in January 1913, these various groups were embodied as the Ulster Volunteer Force. However, despite the weapons to hand and the purchase of additional firearms from England, only a portion of the UVF could be considered to be adequately armed and thus a means was needed to remedy this deficit.

The solution to the problem was as convoluted as it was ingenious. During the summer, a man calling himself John Washington Graham arrived at the London offices of the Vickers Company, enquiring about the purchase of several machine guns. Officials there chose to believe that the weapons were destined for one of the factions in the ongoing civil war in Mexico but, once the transaction was completed, the weapons were taken to Euston Railway Station, where shipment was arranged to Belfast – 'Graham' was in fact Colonel Hugh Crawford, a former artillery officer and now a member of the UVF Headquarters Staff.

Although he had been involved in the procurement of arms for some time, Crawford was aware that the risks inherent in the piecemeal smuggling of weapons and ammunition from Britain were too high and that an alternate source needed to be found. He discovered the answer to his problems in a German arms dealer called Bruno Spiro. Their first attempt at shipping rifles foundered when British customs officials seized a consignment of 400 Italian-made Vetterli rifles in Belfast but, undismayed, a second, larger coup was planned.

Early in 1914 Crawford travelled to Hamburg, where he arranged for the purchase of 20,000 magazine-fed rifles of Austro-German manufacture, complete with bayonets and some two million rounds of ammunition to which consignment was added a number of Vetterlis which had been, for some reason, held back from the previous shipment.

To cover his trail Crawford arranged a series of deceptions that ensured that, once the mission began, he remained incommunicado from his superiors. This proved to be fortuitous as, fearful of intervention by the British Government, a number of senior Unionists – with the notable exception of Carson – were in favour of aborting the enterprise altogether, but were unable to do so whilst they were unsure of Crawford's location.

On the evening of 24 April, the collier *Clyde Valley* made a rendezvous outside the port of Larne and transhipped quantities of rifles and ammunition into several local vessels, which then made subsidiary landings at Bangor, Belfast and Donaghdee. By the following morning the weapons had been unloaded under the noses of local customs inspectors and spirited away to be cached at various locations throughout Ulster.

In London, despite being aware that its policy towards the question of Home Rule was steadily eroding any local support it may have found in Ulster, the Government drafted contingency plans to deploy troops in support of the civil authorities for the process of maintaining law and order. However, there was a canker at the heart of Britain's military apparatus – rather than being apolitical, many senior officers had begun to air their opinions and concerns over Irish affairs, among them the Director of Military Operations, Major-General Sir Henry Wilson, an officer whose family had held land in Co. Antrim for over 200 years.

Wilson had many friends in high places, and when Field Marshal Sir John French, the Chief of the Imperial General Staff, expressed concern that sending troops into Ulster could lead to civil war, Wilson told him 'I could not fire on the North at the dictation of Redmond' and furthermore that 'it will split the Army and the Colonies, as well as the Country and the Empire'. He continued in the same vein to anyone who would listen and then went on to endorse Lord Hugh Cecil's oddly prescient suggestion that, in time of war, Carson should pledge the UVF to serve in the British Army, declaring that it would be the perfect way to place the Government in an impossible position over the deployment of troops in Ulster.

At Westminster, tensions began to rise and in an attempt to defuse the issue Asquith, the Prime Minister, tabled an amendment to the existing bill to allow the Ulster counties to remain outside the framework of Home Rule for a period of up to six years, during which time alternate solutions would be explored. Needless to say, Carson rejected the olive branch outright, demanding that Ulster be 'given a resolution rather than a stay of execution'. This rebuff angered the Government and over the next week plans were made to redeploy troops from various garrisons to occupy strategic positions throughout the province in order to prevent the threatened insurrection and assist in the arrest of a number of prominent Unionists, Carson amongst them.

## THE CURRAGH INCIDENT

As Wilson had foretold, the commanders of the Irish establishment were initially hesitant to follow their orders but Sir Arthur Paget, the commander-in-chief, had managed to secure a concession of sorts from the War Office: officers who were either from or lived in Ulster would be permitted to 'disappear' until the cessation of operations, at which time they would be able to resume their normal duties without a blemish on their career; other officers who declined to follow orders would not be permitted to resign but would instead be dishonourably discharged from the service.

At 0930hrs on 20 March 1914, Paget held the first of two briefings with his senior officers to outline the proposed operations, but made an incalculable error in referring to the Ulster Unionists as if they were a hostile power rather than British citizens. The assembled brigadiers were then informed that their subordinates would have until that evening to decide if they would follow their orders or not and, turning to Brigadier Hubert Gough of the 3rd Cavalry Brigade, Paget gave orders that a squadron of cavalry should be held in immediate readiness for deployment in the North.

As the meeting closed, Gough spoke up and said that he had no ties to Ulster except those of friendship, but was unsure if he could bear arms against the Unionists. Paget retorted that the question of residence would be strictly interpreted and the discussion ended on this further bad note. At the second meeting, held later that afternoon – from which Gough was notably absent – the Government plan was revealed: simply put, various buildings in Belfast were to be occupied to ensure the peace and a further three divisions of troops, together with other supporting formations, would be deployed for a rapid transfer to Ulster should events get out of hand. Even as these preparations were being made the First Sea Lord, Winston Churchill, ordered the 3rd Battle Squadron to Lamlash in the Firth of Clyde, ready to shell Belfast in support of land operations.

As the afternoon briefing continued, Gough was busy discussing the orders with his regimental commanders and, as a result, many of his officers declared that they would resign their commissions rather than march on Ulster making it now certain that the 3rd Cavalry Brigade would not obey any orders to do so. Paget's fear was now how to prevent this disaffection from spreading to other elements of his command and, in an attempt to avoid a fully fledged mutiny, Gough and two of his

Statue of an Irish Volunteer, Royal Canal Bridge, Phibsboro. This statue depicts an Irish Volunteer in full uniform and equipment as prescribed by regulations. In reality few were able to equip themselves with more than a passing nod to the requirements laid down by the Volunteer high command. (Author's collection)

colonels were summoned to a meeting at the War Office in London where Sir John French attempted to smooth matters over. Gough was intransigent until Colonel John Seely, the Secretary of State for War, provided him with a written guarantee that the troops would not be used to force Ulster into an acceptance of Home Rule.

The military may have been mollified but this was not the end of the affair. Asquith took exception to Seely's intervention and a political firestorm erupted in Parliament with the Prime Minister disavowing the guarantee signed by the Secretary of State and the Opposition insinuating that the Government had deliberately set out on a course of incitement to provoke unrest and bloodshed in Ulster, thereby obtaining licence to move overwhelming numbers of troops into the province. This insinuation that would prove well founded as successive weeks found more 'evidence' released through the press, and it was under these conditions that Crawford left for his rendezvous with Benny Spiro in Hamburg.

## A CALL TO ARMS

With the formation of the UVF, the cry went up from many nationalists that a similar body be raised to protect their own interests and, on 25 November 1913, a meeting was held at the Rotunda in Dublin for the express purpose of recruiting a body of men, to be known as the 'National Volunteers'. Chaired by the eminent Gaelic scholar, Professor

Entrance to the Ship Street Barracks. The barracks, adjacent to Dublin Castle, afforded the best immediate protection for the civil administration and was the initial concentration point for British troops in an attempt to stabilize the situation. (Author's collection)

Éoin MacNeill, the gathering soon spilled over into the adjacent public gardens, as thousands turned up to pledge their support.

MacNeill called for solidarity with the Unionists rather than a policy of agitation, but for all this patina of conciliation there were a small number of men who were set on nothing less than armed rebellion to achieve their aims of an independent Ireland: members of the Irish Republican Brotherhood (IRB), the spiritual heirs of the men who had raided Canada in the 1860s and initiated a bombing campaign on the British mainland 20 years later.

Initially they were few in number and, with the exception of Thomas Clarke who had served 15 years in British prisons, relatively unknown; but with his support and patronage they gradually gained importance within the movement, pursuing a hidden agenda that would only become apparent as the events of spring 1916 unfolded.

In London John Redmond saw the formation of the Volunteers as a further opportunity to cement his position as spokesman for nationalism as a whole and discussions were soon under way during the course of which the Volunteer Executive was given a stark choice – either to open its ranks to a number of his nominees or to face boycott and political oblivion. Fierce arguments raged, but in the end Redmond had his way and for the time being it seemed as if all nationalists spoke with same voice.

## THE VOYAGE OF THE *ASGARD*

As 1914 progressed and news of their gun-running exploits became public knowledge, the Irish Volunteers became increasingly obsessed with maintaining some form of balance with the UVF – in the words of Patrick Pearse, 'there is only one thing more comical than a Unionist with a rifle, and that is a Nationalist without one'.

Without the Unionists' financial backers, any attempts by the Volunteers to bring arms into Ireland would be limited by the extent of any funds that could be obtained from well-wishers, but with several private donations they were able to send a journalist named Darrell Figgis to the Continent to procure firearms. In Hamburg, Figgis came into contact with a German arms company named Moritz Magnus that had a number of army surplus weapons for sale, the main problem being that they were being stored near the Belgian city of Liège.

Travelling to Belgium, Figgis reported that, whilst in relatively good condition, the rifles were predominantly obsolete single-shot Mausers, but that for this reason they could be had relatively cheaply, along with a substantial amount of 11mm ammunition.

Constrained by a lack of funds, the Volunteer Executive approved the purchase of 1,500 of these rifles with 49,000 rounds of ammunition, but how could the cargo be safely transported to Ireland? Although the weapons were stored at Liège, the nearby port of Antwerp was out of the question because of the Belgian customs service, and so the only real option was to move them back to Hamburg and arrange for their transfer by sea.

The Irish Volunteers did not lack for members of the calibre of Frederick Crawford and two of these – Erskine Childers and Conor

O'Brien, both renowned amateur yachtsmen – offered their services. The plan was that Childers in his yacht *Asgard* and O'Brien in the *Kelpie* would sail in tandem to a rendezvous near the Ruytigen Lightship in the Scheldt Estuary where they would transfer the arms from a tug chartered by Figgis – each vessel would take half of the cargo and deliver the weapons to prearranged landing points for collection by the Volunteers: Childers would deliver his cargo to the dockside at Howth, north of Dublin, whilst, following further transhipment, O'Brien's weapons would be unloaded at Kilcoole in Co. Wicklow.

Because of storm damage, Childers had to put into Cowes for repairs and sent O'Brien ahead to make the rendezvous with Figgis, following as best he could and meeting the tug on the evening of 12 July. Here, his plans took another blow as the *Kelpie* had taken only a fraction of the weapons aboard, and so after several hours of back-breaking work and lying dangerously low in the water the *Asgard* was towed across the channel by the German tug *Gladiator* laden with 900 Mausers and 29,000 rounds of ammunition.

Things continued to deteriorate; for safety reasons some ammunition that had been stored on deck had to be jettisoned and then *Asgard* sailed into large numbers of British warships en route for the grand review being held at Spithead. Having turned the Lizard, the *Asgard* continued up to Milford Haven in order to disembark one of her crew, a man called Gordon Shephard who was a serving officer in the British Army.

After Milford Haven the *Asgard* made good time until the night of 22 July when she sailed straight into the worst storm to have hit the Irish Sea in decades. Severely battered, Childers ran before the storm towards Holyhead where he remained until the afternoon of Friday 24 July, before deciding to ignore much of the storm damage in an attempt to make the agreed landing at Howth on 26 July.

## THE FIRST SHOTS

Whilst Childers and O'Brien sailed for their rendezvous, plans were being made for the reception of the weapons. Accordingly, Bulmer Hobson, the secretary of the Volunteers arranged for several hundred men to make a route march to Howth on the morning of 26 July, under the cover of which they would accept the *Asgard*'s cargo and bring it to a series of safe houses in Dublin.

It was with a profound sense of relief that the watchers on shore saw the yacht approach the harbour and soon they set to with a will, unloading the cargo and distributing the arms throughout the column before turning back for Dublin.

This sense of well-being was misplaced as, rather than interfering with the Volunteers, the customs officers at Howth had simply telephoned the headquarters of the Dublin Metropolitan Police to give a verbal report on what had transpired.

Deciding to intercept the arms before the Volunteers could disperse in Dublin, Assistant Commissioner Harrel of the DMP set out with a number of policemen to which – albeit by overstepping his authority – he added a detachment of the King's Own Scottish Borderers under the command of a Major Haig. The policemen drew up across the Malahide

Road as the column hove into sight and, in the ensuing scuffle, several men – on both sides – were injured and a number of rifles seized. Bulmer Hobson, along with Darrell Figgis and Thomas MacDonagh, the Volunteers' commander, then attempted to negotiate their way past the roadblock whilst at the same time instructing their rearmost men to scatter and make their way into Dublin.

Seeing his quarry escape before his eyes, Harrel had no option other than to disperse his men and order the troops back to barracks. Returning to Dublin, an increasingly hostile crowd dogged the KOSBs and, as they turned westwards onto Bachelor's Walk, the insults became physical, with stones and brickbats being thrown. In an attempt to halt the abuse, Haig about-turned his rearmost platoons and ordered the men to present arms, hoping that the implied threat would be sufficient to disperse the mob. Somehow the order was misinterpreted and a soldier opened fire, followed by one and then another of his comrades. Then as reflexes took over, a scattered volley rang out killing three and wounding 38, one of whom later died.

Whether the later accusations that a number of the casualties had been bayoneted by the troops can be substantiated remains unclear, but on Bachelor's Walk – much to the satisfaction of the militants within the Irish Volunteers, and given the perceived view that the authorities had turned a blind eye to the Larne gun-running by the UVF – it can be said that the opening shots of the Easter Rising were fired.

# CHRONOLOGY

**1849** End of the Great Famine in Ireland – one million die of hunger and one million emigrate overseas.

**1858** Foundation of the Irish Republican Brotherhood in Dublin.

**1859** Foundation of the Fenian Brotherhood in the United States of America.

**1867** Abortive Fenian Rising in Ireland. Execution of the 'Manchester Martyrs'.

**1868** Gladstone elected British Prime Minister.

**1880** Charles Stewart Parnell becomes leader of Irish Parliamentary Party.

**1885** Gaelic Athletic Association founded.

**1886** First Home Rule Bill defeated in the House of Commons.

**1890** Parnell deposed as leader of Irish Parliamentary Party.

**1893** Second Home Rule Bill passed in the House of Commons, but defeated in House of Lords.
Gaelic League Established.

**1899** Arthur Griffith founds the newspaper *United Irishman*.

**1905** Arthur Griffith founds *Sinn Féin* as a political party.

**1906** Liberal Party wins landslide election victory in Great Britain.

**1908** Foundation of Irish Transport & General Workers Union (ITGWU).

**1910** Two general elections held in Britain – IPP effectively holds balance of power.
Sir Edward Carson elected leader of Ulster Unionists.

**1911** Parliament Act removes power of veto from the House of Lords.

**1912** Third Home Rule Bill passed in House of Commons, House of Lords imposes two-year delay on its implementation as Law.
Unionists sign Solemn League and Covenant.

**1913** *January* – Formation of the UVF.
*April* – UVF lands arms and ammunition at Larne and several other ports.
*November* – Formation of the Irish Volunteers and Irish Citizen Army.
Great Dublin Lockout.

**1914** *March* – Curragh Incident.
*July* – Irish Volunteers land arms and ammunition at Howth.
*August* – Irish Volunteers land arms and ammunition at Kilcoole.
*August* – Outbreak of World War I.
*September* – Third Home Rule Bill enacted as law but suspended for duration of hostilities.
IRB decides upon an uprising against British Rule.
Formation of the Military Council, led by Tom Clarke and Seán MacDermott.

**1916** *January* – Military Council agree on insurrection for Easter Weekend.
*3 April* – Preparation begins for insurrection to take place on 23 April.
*21 April* – *Aud* captured by Royal Navy and scuttles herself off Queenstown.
*22 April* – Éoin MacNeill – IVF Chief of Staff – issues countermand order to stop Rising.
*24 April* – Beginning of the Easter Rising.
*29 April* – Patrick Pearse signs instrument of unconditional surrender. Fighting ends.
*May* – Trial of the participants in the Rising by field general court martial.
Execution of the leaders of the Rising and internment of other participants.
*July* – Battle of the Somme.
*August* – Sir Roger Casement hanged in London.
*December* – Release of the first prisoners from internment in Great Britain.

**1917** *July* – Release of remaining prisoners held in British prisons/internment camps.
Eamon de Valera elected to Parliament in East Clare by-election.

# THE OPPOSING COMMANDERS

## THE REBELS

A t the heart of the Rising lay not an officer of the Volunteers nor of the Citizen Army, but a small group of activists, members of the supposedly defunct Irish Republican Brotherhood who, whilst ostensibly serving as members of the Volunteer Movement, had clandestinely promoted their own plans for an armed rebellion against British rule. Known simply as the Military Council this small group of men had, from its inception, concentrated their efforts on the manipulation of the Volunteer Movement.

Arguably the most influential member of the Council was Thomas James Clarke, who had emigrated to America in 1880 at the age of 23 to work in the construction industry. A scant three years later, Clarke was sent to Britain as part of a Republican bombing campaign, but was arrested and sentenced to 15 years in prison where he and his co-prisoners were subjected to continued mental and physical torture by their guards. Under a harsh regime, exemplified by beatings, starvation, sleep deprivation and impromptu punishments such as being forced to stand on a house-brick for up to 24 hours at a time, many of Clarke's contemporaries either went insane or attempted suicide as a means of escape. Clarke, however, retreated into himself and, on his release in 1898, he returned to America where he became the main link between *Clann na Gael* – the most influential Republican organization – and the IRB. Becoming disillusioned with his own generation of Republicans, whom he chided as having become too conservative, Clarke came into ever closer contact with the more radical members of the IRB and struck up friendships with two of the more prominent: John Bulmer Hobson and Seán MacDermott, both in their mid-20s and committed to an insurrection against British rule, irrespective of the cost. And so, by 1912, all three were members of that body's Supreme Council; to all intents and purposes the militants were in control of the Brotherhood, but where would they lead it?

The formation of the Irish Volunteers in November 1913, as a counterbalance to the UVF, and the passive acceptance of John Redmond's seizure of control of the organization proved to be another turning point, for Hobson seemingly repudiated his allies and sided with those moderates who viewed Redmondite interference as the lesser of two evils when compared to the likely breakup of the Volunteers, a fragmentation which took place scant months later when Redmond made a public speech calling for the Volunteers to

Printed copy of the proclamation of the Irish Republic. In order to maintain secrecy, the proclamation of the Republic was produced on a hand press in Liberty Hall a few hours before the Rising. Produced in two sections, a shortage of lettering meant that the letter 'e' had to be improvised, standing out from the rest of the text. (Courtesy National Museum of Ireland, Dublin – HE4474/B195)

---

**POBLACHT NA H EIREANN.**

**THE PROVISIONAL GOVERNMENT**

OF THE

**IRISH REPUBLIC**

**TO THE PEOPLE OF IRELAND.**

IRISHMEN AND IRISHWOMEN : In the name of God and of the dead generations from which she receives her old tradition of nationhood, Ireland, through us, summons her children to her flag and strikes for her freedom.

Having organised and trained her manhood through her secret revolutionary organisation, the Irish Republican Brotherhood, and through her open military organisations, the Irish Volunteers and the Irish Citizen Army, having patiently perfected her discipline, having resolutely waited for the right moment to reveal itself, she now seizes that moment, and, supported by her exiled children in America and by gallant allies in Europe, but relying in the first on her own strength, she strikes in full confidence of victory.

We declare the right of the people of Ireland to the ownership of Ireland, and to the unfettered control of Irish destinies, to be sovereign and indefeasible. The long usurpation of that right by a foreign people and government has not extinguished the right, nor can it ever be extinguished except by the destruction of the Irish people. In every generation the Irish people have asserted their right to national freedom and sovereignty : six times during the past three hundred years they have asserted it in arms. Standing on that fundamental right and again asserting it in arms in the face of the world, we hereby proclaim the Irish Republic as a Sovereign Independent State, and we pledge our lives and the lives of our comrades-in-arms to the cause of its freedom, of its welfare, and of its exaltation among the nations.

The Irish Republic is entitled to, and hereby claims, the allegiance of every Irishman and Irishwoman. The Republic guarantees religious and civil liberty, equal rights and equal opportunities to all its citizens, and declares its resolve to pursue the happiness and prosperity of the whole nation and of all its parts, cherishing all the children of the nation equally, and oblivious of the differences carefully fostered by an alien government, which have divided a minority from the majority in the past.

Until our arms have brought the opportune moment for the establishment of a permanent National Government, representative of the whole people of Ireland and elected by the suffrages of all her men and women, the Provisional Government, hereby constituted, will administer the civil and military affairs of the Republic in trust for the people.

We place the cause of the Irish Republic under the protection of the Most High God, Whose blessing we invoke upon our arms, and we pray that no one who serves that cause will dishonour it by cowardice, inhumanity, or rapine. In this supreme hour the Irish nation must, by its valour and discipline and by the readiness of its children to sacrifice themselves for the common good, prove itself worthy of the august destiny to which it is called.

Signed on behalf of the Provisional Government,

THOMAS J. CLARKE.
SEAN Mac DIARMADA, THOMAS MacDONAGH.
P. H. PEARSE, EAMONN CEANNT.
JAMES CONNOLLY. JOSEPH PLUNKETT.

---

# IRISH REPUBLICAN ARMY

## Leaders in the Insurrection, May, 1916

*IRISH REBELLION, MAY 1916.*     *IRISH REBELLION, MAY, 1916.*     *IRISH REBELLION, MAY 1916.*     *IRISH REBELLION, MAY, 1916.*

THOMAS MacDONAGH.
(Commandant of Stephen's Street Area).
Executed May 3rd, 1916.
One of the signatories of the "Irish Republic Proclamation."

J. J. HEUSTON,
One of the leaders of the Rebellion.
Executed May 8th, 1916.

CORNELIUS COLBERT.
(Who took a prominent part in the Rebellion).
Executed May 8th, 1916.

SEAN MAC DIARMADA.
Executed May 9th, 1916.
One of the signatories of the "Irish Republic Proclamation."

*IRISH REBELLION, MAY 1916*     *IRISH REBELLION, MAY 1916.*     *IRISH REBELLION, MAY 1916*     *IRISH REBELLION, MAY 1916.*

THE O'RAHILLY.
One of the Leaders, who was Shot in Action, G.P.O. Area.

MAJOR JOHN McBRIDE.
(Born in Westport, May 7th, 1865).
Executed in Kilmainham Prison, May 5th, 1916.

P. H. PEARSE.
(Commandant-General of the Army of the Irish Republic).
Executed May 3rd, 1916.
One of the signatories of the "Irish Republic Proclamation."

JAMES CONNOLLY.
(Commandant-General, Dublin Division).
Executed May 9th, 1916.
One of the signatories of the "Irish Republic Proclamation."

*IRISH REBELLION, MAY 1916*     *IRISH REBELLION, MAY 1916*     *IRISH REBELLION, MAY 1916*     *IRISH REBELLION, MAY 1916.*

THOMAS ASHE.
(Leader of the North County Dublin Volunteers in the Rising).
Sentenced to Death:
Sentence commuted to Penal Servitude for Life.

E. DALY.
(Commandant of the North-West Dublin Area).
Executed May 4th, 1916.

EAMONN CEANNT.
(Commandant of the South Dublin Area).
Executed May 8th, 1916.
One of the signatories of the "Irish Republic Proclamation."

COUNTESS MARKIEVICZ.
(Who took a prominent part in the Rebellion, Stephen's Green Area).
Sentenced to Death:
Sentence commuted to Penal Servitude for Life.

*IRISH REBELLION, MAY 1916.*     *IRISH REBELLION, MAY 1916.*     *IRISH REBELLION, MAY 1916.*     *IRISH REBELLION, MAY 1916.*

MICHAEL O'HANRAHAN.
(Author of "The Swordsmen of the Brigade," etc.).
Executed in Kilmainham Prison, May 4th, 1916.

ED. de VALERA.
(Commandant of the Ringsend Area).
Sentenced to Death:
Sentence commuted to Penal Servitude for Life.

THOMAS J. CLARKE.
Executed May 3rd, 1916.
One of the signatories of the "Irish Republic Proclamation."

JOSEPH PLUNKETT, (son of Count Plunkett),
Commandant-General Irish Republican Army,
Executed May 4th, 1916.
Who was married a few hours before his execution.

Printed and Published by the Powell Press, 22 Parliament Street, Dublin.

enlist in the British Army. The overwhelming majority seemed to heed the rallying call, renaming themselves the 'National' Volunteers whilst very much the rump, some 13,000 men, intended to remain firmly aloof from such involvement as the 'Irish' Volunteers.

It was an interesting quandary – the moderates maintaining that a movement 'in being' would deter Britain from either a partition of Ireland or the imposition of conscription, whilst the IRB saw it as a revolutionary army which should be used against Britain at the earliest opportunity. This was the perfect situation for Clarke to oust Hobson from the Supreme Council, and to begin planning for the Rising which, for him, was both inevitable and irrevocable.

The plan called for the establishment of a Military Council, which – given the IRB's obsession with secrecy – would consist of three men whose task would be to draft the plans for an insurrection and, some time in early 1915, Clarke and MacDermott had found their recruits: Patrick Henry Pearse, Joseph Mary Plunkett and Eamonn Céannt, respectively the Volunteers' directors of organization, operations and communications. In one fell swoop, the IRB had driven a wedge between the Volunteer Executive and the rank and file for no orders would be dispatched by Éoin MacNeill, the Volunteers' chief of staff, without first passing through the hands of the Military Council.

With the addition of Clarke and MacDermott as ex officio members, the composition of the Military Council remained identical until April 1916 when, shortly before the Rising, James Connolly, leader of the IGTWU and commander of the Irish Citizen Army, and Thomas MacDonagh, commander of the 2nd (Dublin City) Battalion of the Irish Volunteers, were admitted to the Council, and these seven men were to form the Provisional Government of the Irish Republic.

# THE BRITISH

### Lieutenant-General Sir John Grenfell Maxwell – GOC Ireland

Born in 1859, Maxwell received his lieutenant's commission in July 1881, serving with the 1st Battalion, Black Watch, during the Egyptian War of 1882, and was decorated following the battle of Tel El-Kebir in 1882.

During the 1885/6 Sudan campaign, he was appointed as ADC to General Grenfell – a distant relative – and was mentioned in dispatches on several occasions. At the end of the campaign he transferred to the Egyptian Army, being promoted to captain and appointed as an ADC to the Sirdar or C.-in-C. of the Egyptian Forces – Horatio Herbert, Lord Kitchener – an appointment that would have a direct bearing on Maxwell's role in the pacification of Ireland in 1916.

In 1896 he was given the command of the 3rd Egyptian Brigade for the Dongola campaign and promoted to brevet lieutenant-colonel, but the following year he returned to Army HQ as assistant military secretary to Lord Kitchener and served in this role until April 1900, when he transferred to South Africa, being eventually appointed to the command of the 7th Division's 14th Infantry Brigade. In 1901, he was appointed military governor of Pretoria, ending the war as GOC North-West Transvaal, being created KCB and CMG.

Lieutenant-General Sir John Maxwell. Although appointed C.-in-C. Ireland shortly after the outset of the Rising, Maxwell only assumed personal command on Friday 28 April, leaving Lowe in charge of operations. His main source of 'infamy' lies in his handling of the trial and subsequent execution of the Rebel leaders. (Courtesy the *Illustrated London News*)

Broadsheet published in Dublin showing 16 portraits of the Rebel leaders. Of the subjects, the O'Rahilly was the only one to be killed in action, whilst Ashe, Markiewicz and de Valera all received prison sentences. The remainder, with the inclusion of Willie Pearse and Michael Mallin, were executed at Kilmainham Jail between 3 and 12 May. (Courtesy Imperial War Museum, London – Q70583)

Maxwell was then promoted to staff brigadier of III Army Corps in Ireland where he remained until May 1904. Two years later he was promoted to major-general and, in 1907, was appointed as chief staff officer for the Mediterranean Command, a position held until September 1908 when he became GOC Egypt, receiving his promotion to lieutenant-general on 4 September 1912. The outbreak of hostilities in August 1914 saw Maxwell transferred to the Western Front as chief liaison officer to the French Army, but this role was short lived and he returned to Egypt in September of that year.

The outbreak of the Easter Rising found Sir John Maxwell in London recuperating from a minor operation, when he received a summons from his old commander, Lord Kitchener, who was now Minister for War.

Having disregarded the nomination of General Sir Ian Hamilton on the grounds of the excessive Irish casualties that had been suffered during the ill-fated Dardanelles campaign, Kitchener offered Maxwell the job of suppressing the Rising and pacifying Ireland. It was to be a fateful choice.

### Brigadier W. H. M. Lowe – CO 3rd Reserve Cavalry Brigade

Lowe's early career followed an almost parallel path to that of the man who would be his commanding officer in 1916. Like Maxwell, he joined the army in 1881 and received his baptism of fire during the 1882 Egyptian campaign. His next posting saw him transferred to the headquarters staff for the Burma expedition of 1886/7, after which he returned to regimental service.

1899 saw Lowe promoted to lieutenant-colonel of the 7th Dragoon Guards during the Boer War, where his aggressive tactics brought him to the notice of his senior officers and resulted in his being mentioned in dispatches on several occasions.

By the time of the Easter Rising, Lowe was in command of the 3rd Reserve Cavalry Brigade, a training formation based at the Curragh Camp in Co. Kildare, west of Dublin. It was the qualities which had been recognized in South Africa, in contrast with those of his nominal superior, Major-General Sir Lovick Friend, which allowed the British forces to weather the initial attacks and consolidate their positions to contain and defeat the Rebel forces.

### Colonel Ernest William Stuart King Maconchy – CO 178th Brigade, 59th Division

Commissioned in 1882, Lieutenant Maconchy first saw active service in India during the Hazara expedition of 1888, where he was to receive the DSO following a night action at Ghazikot, during which his command held off a surprise attack by several hundred native warriors. For the next decade he saw almost continuous active service along the North-West Frontier of India, eventually being brevetted as major.

Maconchy served in South Africa with the Indian Staff Corps, but returned to India to take part in the Waziristan expedition of 1901, during which his rank of major was confirmed. He then held several staff appointments before being given command of the 51st Sikhs in 1904. Further staff roles followed his promotion to colonel, and he retired from the Indian Service in January 1914. The following year, he came out of retirement to accept command of the 178th Brigade of the 59th Division, leading that formation during the Easter Rising.

# OPPOSING ARMIES

## THE REBELS

Following the enrolment en masse of significant numbers of Volunteers in November 1913, the Executive needed to reorganize on a national level both formally and with regard to training. As such, by 1914 it was agreed that they would adopt contemporary British practice, one consideration being the significant number of former British soldiers available as potential officers and drill instructors whilst a second, equally important, factor was the widespread availability in Dublin's booksellers of the British Infantry Training Manual for 1911.

Organization again followed British lines with a battalion, under the command of a colonel, comprising eight companies – lettered A to H – each of 79 officers and men, and a variable number of supernumeraries giving a unit strength of up to 650 effectives. Initially several such battalions grouped around a single recruitment area were combined to form a regiment for example the 'Dublin City Regiment' under the command of a senior colonel, but some time during 1915, these terms were phased out, being replaced with 'brigade' and 'commandant' respectively. Additionally, and by the time of the Easter Rising, in order to absorb the 'losses' caused by defections to John Redmond's 'National Volunteers' it is likely that the units of the Dublin City brigade had been reorganized on a reduced, six-company basis, lettered A to F.

In August 1914, the Volunteers decided upon an official uniform of grey-green woollen serge, comprising a tunic, two-button breeches and semi-spiral puttees; headdress varied, ranging from a Boer-style slouch

Mobilization order, 4th (City of Dublin Battalion) Irish Volunteers. This order for C Company of Céannt's 4th Battalion was to have been issued on Easter Sunday. Following the 'Countermand Order' the Rising was delayed until Easter Monday, an event that undoubtedly contributed to the Rebels' initial successes. (Courtesy National Museum of Ireland, Dublin – HE1180/B273)

hat to an unstiffened peaked cap. Original uniform samples were ordered from an English military contractor and presented to various Irish manufacturers to see if they could produce similar items – in one of those odd twists of fate, several military outfitters in Dublin were soon supplying both the Volunteers and members of the British Army with their equipment. This fact notwithstanding, the majority of the rank and file went into action with a bandolier and rifle as their sole aspect of uniform.

Within the Volunteer 'umbrella' were three additional groups: a woman's auxiliary body, the *Cumann na mBan*; a youth movement, the *Fianna*; and the Volunteer Auxiliary, whose members were unable to commit the required amount of time to training, but were expected to learn marksmanship and basic military skills.

Fighting alongside the Volunteers were the smaller Irish Citizen Army, a body of men organized by James Connolly in the wake of the Great Dublin Lockout of 1913, with the sole purpose of protecting trade union members from the attentions of either the police or enforcers employed by the factory owners with whom Connolly's IGTWU was often at loggerheads. The ICA wore a uniform of similar cut to the Volunteers, albeit of a darker colour cloth, whilst the brims on their slouch hats were pinned up with a badge in the shape of the red hand of Ulster.

In order to arm themselves, the Volunteers resorted to various legal and illegal methods, which resulted in the plethora of weapon types retrieved after the Rising: British service rifles were obtained either by theft or purchase from soldiers on leave who then reported the weapons as having been stolen, whilst sporting rifles and shotguns were purchased 'over the counter' by 'persons of good standing' and then passed on to the Volunteers. Additionally, when import restrictions were lifted following Britain's declaration of war against Germany, direct contact was made with British armaments factories, such as Greener & Co of Birmingham, and in this way several thousand rifles were obtained on the open market.

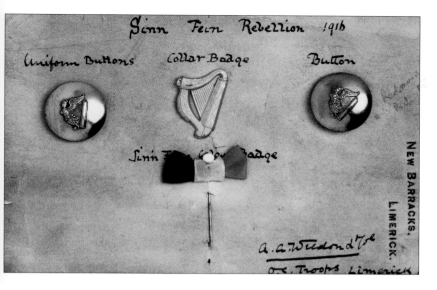

In the image, handwritten text reads:

Sinn Fein Rebellion 1916
Uniform Buttons    Collar Badge    Button
Sinn Fein Cap Badge
a. a. Weldon d 7th
o.c. Troops Limerick
NEW BARRACKS, LIMERICK.

*Sinn Feín* **badges and collar buttons. These are early examples of Volunteer brass uniform insignia. Later regulations insisted that buttons should be either covered in leather or darkened. (Courtesy Imperial War Museum, London – MH33675)**

However, the weapon that has come to symbolize the Irish Volunteers is the 'Howth' rifle, so named after the port where the *Asgard* landed some 900 such rifles in July 1914. Although it is possible that more than one type of rifle was landed at Howth, the predominant weapon is generally accepted as being an early model Mauser rifle – most likely the M1871 – a single-shot weapon firing an 11mm round propelled by a charge of slow-burning black powder, which gave the weapon a fierce recoil. Because of this, it was loudly – and erroneously – condemned by Patrick Pearse as being both antiquated and contrary to the Hague Conventions, which then led many British observers to claim that the Volunteers used either dumdum or exploding cartridges during the Rising.

# THE BRITISH

Upon the outbreak of war in 1914, Ireland's 'Regular' garrison units were transferred overseas with their places being taken by 'Reserve' or 'third-line' formations whose unit titles bore such descriptions as 'Reserve', 'Extra-Reserve' or 'Service', and whose chief purpose was to provide cadres of trained recruits for their first- and second-line parent formations. As far as can be ascertained, the organization was such that the 15th (Ulster) Reserve Infantry Brigade, responsible for the north of Ireland, was based in Belfast, with the 25th (Irish) Reserve Infantry Brigade being based at the Curragh, and responsible for the middle of the country as well as the garrisoning of Dublin. A third reserve brigade was based in and around Cork.

In 1915, infantry battalions were reorganized on a five-company basis – a headquarters company and four rifle companies, lettered A–D, each comprising some 200 effectives for a battalion strength of 1,000 officers and men. However, if we compare this, for example, with the troop returns for the three infantry battalions in Dublin on 24 April 1916, we can see how chronically under strength these formations were, not just in terms of common soldiers but, more importantly, in terms of experienced officers and NCOs.

**Private Ivor Evans, 2nd Battalion, the Prince of Wales' Leinster Regiment. Forming part of the 25th Reserve Infantry Brigade, the Leinsters were initially used to screen Eamonn Céannt's forces in the South Dublin Union before pushing forward to reinforce the garrison of Dublin Castle. (Courtesy Imperial War Museum, London – HU93410)**

2nd Lieutenant Basil Green, 5th Battalion, the North Staffordshire Regiment. Following the capture of the Mount Street Canal Bridge, the Staffordshire Brigade (177th) contained de Valera's 3rd Volunteer battalion, before opening up the direct route into the city and relieving the garrison of Trinity College (Courtesy Imperial War Museum, London – HU93421)

Lieutenant Arthur Wills, 9th Battalion, the Sherwood Foresters. Although not present in Ireland, this portrait shows in detail the insignia of the Sherwood Foresters. (Courtesy Imperial War Museum, London – HU93586)

This lack of leadership would be partially offset by the numbers of men from other regiments who were in Dublin, either on detachment from their parent units or on leave, and subsequently reported for duty, but in tense combat situations, the presence of strange and unknown officers could, and indeed did, have the most tragic of outcomes with at least two being shot by men under their command on suspicion of being either rebels or sympathetic to the rebels.

The remaining formations were the 5th Reserve Artillery Brigade at Athlone, which would send a section of four guns to assist in the suppression of the Rising, and the 3rd Reserve Cavalry Brigade based at the Curragh. With its peculiar organization and composition, this latter formation deserves further review.

Like its infantry counterparts, the 3rd Reserve Cavalry Brigade was primarily a training formation, but differed in the fact that instead of supplying trained recruits for a battalion within the same regiment, each of the reserve cavalry regiments incorporated the training squadrons of several individual units, which were then rotated through basic training before being returned to their parent formation and thus regimental strength fluctuated greatly.

There are, however, two facets of the reserve cavalry that continue to cause confusion. Firstly, the squadrons were not grouped by type or parent formation thus any subunit could consist of a mixture of lancers and yeomanry, which has given rise to some modern works stating that Lt. Hunter's escort troop intended for the Magazine Fort on the afternoon of 24 April were armed with lances whilst others state that they were not – in fact all are technically correct. The final complication of the reserve cavalry TO&E is that as these were temporary formations their members are almost invariably referred to as being a member of their parent unit rather than the relevant training regiment, thus a memorial plaque in the grounds of Trinity College refers to Trooper Arthur Charles Smith of the 4th Hussars, rather than the 10th Reserve Cavalry Regiment with which he actually served during the Rising.

Once it became apparent that additional forces would be required to put down the rebellion, the Imperial General Staff gave orders for elements of the 59th Division, which was designated as the 'reaction

LEFT **Lewis-gun section, 2/6th Sherwood Foresters, Cassiobury Park, Watford. The battalion Lewis-gun section poses for the camera shortly before being sent to Ireland. The size of the unit contradicts the common assumption that the weapons were simply left behind at the behest of an overzealous staff officer. (Courtesy Imperial War Museum, London – Q70686)**

RIGHT **the officers of the North Midland Field Ambulance Section, 59th Division, pose for the camera giving a clear depiction of uniform and rank distinctions. (Courtesy Imperial War Museum, London – Q90436)**

force' for the Home Army and as such deployed in cantonments across the rail network north of London, to entrain for Liverpool to take ship for Ireland. A 'territorial division', the 59th had been formed at the beginning of 1915 but it was still undergoing training at all levels early in 1916, at which time much of its elderly inventory was replaced by more modern equipment.

# ORDERS OF BATTLE

### REBEL FORCES IN DUBLIN – APRIL 1916
Commandant General and Commander-in-Chief of Irish Volunteers – P. H. Pearse
Commandant General and Commander Dublin Division Irish Volunteers – J. Connolly
Commandant General – J. M. Plunkett

### Composite Headquarters Battalion
Muster point       Liberty Hall (Beresford Place) then General Post Office, Sackville Street
Muster       150 men (then reports of increases up to 350 men inc. late arrivals/stragglers)

### 1st (Dublin City) Battalion Irish Volunteers (less D Company)
Commandant – E. Daly
Vice-Commandant – P. Beaslai
Muster point – Blackhall Street
Muster – 250 men

### D Company, 1st (Dublin City) Battalion Irish Volunteers
Commandant – S. Heuston, Captain, D Company, 1st (Dublin City) Battalion, Irish Volunteers
Muster Point – Mountjoy Square
Muster – 12 men

### 2nd (Dublin City) Battalion Irish Volunteers
Commandant – T. MacDonagh, Commander Dublin Brigade Irish Volunteers
Vice-Commandant – J. MacBride, Major
Muster point – St Stephen's Green*
Muster – 200 men

### 3rd (Dublin City) Battalion Irish Volunteers
Commandant – E. de Valera, Adjutant Dublin Brigade Irish Volunteers.
Muster point – Brunswick Street (Also Earlsfort Terrace and Oakley Road)
Muster – 130 men

### 4th (Dublin City) Battalion Irish Volunteers
Commandant – E. Céannt
Vice-Commandant – C. Brugha
Muster point – Emerald Square (nr. Dolphin's Barn)
Muster – 100 men

### 5th (North Dublin) Battalion Irish Volunteers
Commandant – T. Ashe
Muster point – Knocksedan (nr. Swords)
Muster – 60 men

### Irish Citizen Army
Commandant – M. Mallin
Deputy to Michael Mallin – Constance, Countess Markievicz
Muster point – Liberty Hall (Beresford Place)
Muster – 100

### Irish Citizen Army (detachment)
Captain – S. Connolly
Muster point – Liberty Hall (Beresford Place)
Muster – 30 men

### Kimmage Garrison:
Captain – G. Plunkett
Muster point – Kimmage, Plunkett family estate
Muster – 56 men

The best estimate is therefore that, at approximately 1200hrs on 24 April 1916, Rebel forces in Dublin and its surrounding area totalled some 1,100 men (excluding volunteers from the *Fianna* and *Cumann na mBan*), which over the course of the following days would rise to about 1,500 with the inclusion of stragglers etc.

* This was a change from the normal muster point of Father Matthew Park in Fairview to the north-east of the city. When a number of volunteers turned up at the original muster point following the commencement of hostilities, they were then directed to the GPO Building in Sackville Street.


## BRITISH ORDER OF BATTLE – DUBLIN 1916
### Dublin Garrison – Col. Kennard
Marlborough Barracks, Phoenix Park – 6th Reserve Cavalry Regiment (Ex-3rd Reserve Cavalry Bde.) – 35 officers and 851 other ranks. (5th/12th Lancers, City of London/1st County of London Yeomanry)
Portobello Barracks – 3rd (Reserve) Battalion, Royal Irish Rifles – 21 officers and 650 other ranks
Richmond Barracks – 3rd (Reserve) Battalion, Royal Irish Regiment (Lt. Col. R. L. Owens) – 18 officers and 385 other ranks
Royal Barracks – 10th (Service) Battalion, Royal Dublin Fusiliers – 37 officers and 430 other ranks

### The Curragh Camp – Col. (temp Brig.) W. H. M. Lowe:
*Elements 25th Reserve Infantry Brigade*
5th (Extra Reserve) Battalion, Royal Dublin Fusiliers
5th (Extra Reserve) Battalion, The Prince of Wales' Leinster Regiment
*3rd Reserve Cavalry Brigade – Col. Portal*
8th Reserve Cavalry Regiment (16th/17th Lancers, King Edward's Horse, Dorsetshire/Oxfordshire Yeomanry)
9th Reserve Cavalry Regiment (3rd/7th Hussars, 2nd/3rd County of London Yeomanry)

10th Reserve Cavalry Regiment (4th/8th Hussars, Lancashire Hussars, Duke of Lancaster's/Westmoreland/Cumberland Yeomanry)

### Athlone
5th Reserve Artillery Brigade – eight 18-pdr field guns (Only four artillery pieces were found to be serviceable)

### Belfast
Composite Infantry Battalion (drawn from elements of 15th Reserve Infantry Bde.) – 1,000 all ranks

### Templemore
4th (Extra Reserve) Battalion, Royal Dublin Fusiliers (Ex-25th Reserve Infantry Bde.)

### 59th (2nd North Midland) Division – Maj. Gen. A. Sandbach
B Squadron, the North Irish Horse
59th (2/1st North Midland) Divisional Cyclist Company
C Squadron, 2/1st Northumberland Hussars
59th Divisional Signal Company
*176th Infantry Brigade (2nd Lincoln & Leicester) Brig. C. G. Blackader*
2/4th Battalion, the Lincolnshire Regiment
2/5th Battalion, the Lincolnshire Regiment
2/4th Battalion, the Leicestershire Regiment
2/5th Battalion, the Leicestershire Regiment
*177th Infantry Brigade (2nd Staffordshire) Brig. L. R. Carleton*
2/5th Battalion, the South Staffordshire Regiment
2/6th Battalion, the South Staffordshire Regiment
2/5th Battalion, the North Staffordshire Regiment
2/6th Battalion, the North Staffordshire Regiment
*178th Infantry Brigade (2nd Nottingham & Derby) Col. E. W. S. K. Maconchy*
2/5th Battalion, the Sherwood Foresters
2/6th Battalion, the Sherwood Foresters
2/7th Battalion, the Sherwood Foresters – 'The Robin Hoods'
2/8th Battalion, the Sherwood Foresters

295th Brigade, Royal Field Artillery
296th Brigade, Royal Field Artillery
297th Brigade, Royal Field Artillery
298th Brigade, Royal Field Artillery (H)
59th Divisional Ammunition Column
467th Field Company, Royal Engineers
469th Field Company, Royal Engineers
470th Field Company, Royal Engineers
2/1st North Midland Field Ambulance
2/2nd North Midland Field Ambulance
2/3rd North Midland Field Ambulance
59th Divisional Train, Army Service Corps
59th Mobile Veterinary Section
59th (North Midland) Sanitary Section

### Miscellaneous units
Trinity College, OTC
Detachment, Army School of Musketry – Dollymount (Maj. H. F. Somerville)
Home Defence Force 'Georgius Rex'

# OPPOSING PLANS

## THE REBELS

t is often said that 'the enemy of my enemy is my ally', and so it was that, as the troops marched off to war, the Irish Rebels found an unlikely ally in Imperial Germany, with the contact being brokered by the *Clann na Gael*, an Irish-American Republican movement.

The Volunteers' choice of envoy was, on the face of it, a good one – Roger David Casement – a former member of the British Colonial Service. He had been knighted for his work in exposing the cruelties experienced by native workers in the Belgian Congo and thus enjoyed a positive reputation in international circles.

Front, or Parliament, Square of Trinity College looking towards the main gate. Like Dublin Castle, Trinity College was inadequately garrisoned during the early stages of the Rising, and its capture by the insurgents would have given them a much-needed bastion, offsetting the inevitable British superiority in numbers. (Courtesy David Murphy)

The State Apartments, Dublin Castle. It was here, during a meeting about the best way to suppress the Irish Volunteers, that the Government became painfully aware of the Rising, as members of the Citizen Army launched an abortive attempt on the castle gates. (Courtesy David Murphy)

A sketch of Dublin during the Rising. This contemporary drawing shows how the fighting was depicted in the British press. (Courtesy the *Illustrated London News*)

After meeting with the German ambassador to the United States, the *Clann* secured letters of introduction for Casement and arranged for him to travel to Berlin to meet representatives of the German Government.

On 31 October 1914, he arrived in the German capital and was successful in obtaining not only the agreed declaration, but a 'Treaty between Germany and the Irish People' in which it was agreed that an 'Irish Brigade' would be raised from men held in German POW camps; such troops being maintained by Irish sources and – if possible – sent to Ireland with German logistical support. Failing this last, they would be transported either to Egypt to assist the anti-British elements there or to the neutral United States.

Both sides felt that they had brokered a good deal. Ireland would receive a body of well-trained and, presumably, well-armed men to fight against Britain, whilst Germany would drive a wedge between one of the leading Allied Powers and one of her principal sources of recruits. However, Casement soon had doubts about this latter part of his mission as by early 1915, only 50 or so men had volunteered for the Brigade – mainly lured by the prospect of better conditions rather than by any political idealism. Shortly after his arrival, Casement was joined by Joseph Plunkett, who had been sent by the IRB's Supreme Council to 'assist' in negotiations with the German Government.

Together, they came up with several proposals with which the Kaiser's Government could help the rebels, the most audacious of which was for the transfer of a force of several thousand German troops around the

Detail of the Upper Gate, Dublin Castle. As the Citizen Army seized the guardhouse – seen here through the gate, on the left – the gate itself was slammed shut and secured, thus robbing them of the opportunity of seizing the symbol of British rule even as the Republic was being proclaimed. (Courtesy David Murphy)

north coast of Scotland to be landed on Ireland's west coast. At the same time, the Volunteers in and around Dublin would rise against the British who, with their attention thus polarized, would be unable to prevent the invaders from moving inland and securing the 'line of the Shannon'. From there it would be a simple matter of picking off isolated British garrisons before a decisive encounter, which would be fought in terrain inhibitive to the cavalry who, they informed the Germans, formed the bulk of the British Army in Ireland.

The plan was simple, but had a fatal flaw in that they were unable to explain how the Imperial Navy would be able to transport the invasion force past Scapa Flow – the wartime station of Britain's Grand Fleet – without risking the pride of the Kaiser's Navy. As fate would have it, the two fleets were destined to meet at the battle of Jutland/Skaggerak on 31 May 1916, almost a month after the collapse of the Easter Rising.

A modified, scaled-down version of the plan was then submitted that would involve the transfer of the Irish Brigade with a number of German 'advisers' to Ireland, with an agreed cargo of arms and ammunition. Having captured vast amounts of *matériel* during the early battles on the Eastern Front, the Germans had a large supply of surplus weapons that could be used to equip the Volunteers, but were wary of committing themselves to the inclusion of their military personnel in any such adventure.

The strain was proving too much for Casement who went to a Munich sanatorium suffering from nervous exhaustion whereas, with his mission achieved, Plunkett returned to Ireland in order to make arrangements for the anticipated landing. His place was taken by Robert Monteith, a former British soldier, whose job was now to assist in the final training of the Irish Brigade.

Despondent at what he saw as German duplicity Casement began to retreat into himself and, as Monteith had by now shouldered the burden of running the unit, he now began to think in terms of how to abort his mission and avoid an unnecessary waste of lives. Meanwhile, Plunkett's return to Ireland was hailed as a success by his colleagues within the IRB. The agreement with Germany meant that plans for an insurrection could begin in earnest and, in January 1916, a possible threat to their plans was neutralized when they secured the services of probably the most effective of the Rebel leaders during the Rising – James Connolly. The leader of the ITGWU and de facto head of the Citizen Army had declared for some time that his men would take up arms against the British regime in Dublin, irrespective of the Volunteers' intentions and so, fearful that Connolly would compromise their plans, they arranged for him to be kidnapped and taken to a safe house where, for the next few days, intense negotiations went on between the captive and his captors. In the end Connolly was convinced by their arguments and was admitted to the Council, pledging the support of the Citizen Army to the proposed insurrection.

The signal for rebellion would be the mobilization of the Volunteers' 3,500-strong Dublin Brigade, who would secure a series of strategic buildings in Dublin and invite attack, thus drawing British troops towards the east and away from Fenit, Co. Kerry, where the German convoy was due to land sometime between 20 and 23 April.

Of the estimated 13,000 Volunteers in the provinces, the Cork, Kerry, Limerick and Galway Brigades were to deploy in order to cover the initial landings and then move towards the Shannon, whilst the remainder of the Irish Volunteers would adopt a guerrilla role – the Ulster companies were ordered to march westwards to link up with the forces from Galway but were strongly admonished not to provoke or interfere with either British Army units or the UVF whilst on the march.

Given the landing of a significant force of trained troops and a large number of modern weapons Plunkett, and indeed it would appear the whole of the IRB Supreme Council, believed that many if not all of the recently formed 'National Volunteers' would turn their backs on John Redmond and join the Rising, thereby giving the 'Volunteers' a significant numerical edge over the British forces in Ireland. An additional consideration which may have featured in Plunkett's later calculations was the titanic struggle for the French fortress of Verdun, which had been raging since 21 February 1916. A significant break-through by the German Army would critically alter the position on the Western Front – this threat being in itself the catalyst for the impending British Somme Offensive of July 1916 – and the question must be asked could, or indeed, would Britain have sent a major force to Ireland to put down a rebellion, whilst ignoring French cries for support and assistance?

Dublin Castle, former headquarters of G Division, Dublin Metropolitan Police. The armed detectives of G Division were charged with countering political unrest in the city and singularly failed to disrupt the nationalists' plans. (Courtesy David Murphy)

# THE BRITISH

During the evening of Easter Sunday, 23 April, the British authorities finally agreed to measures that would neutralize the nationalist agitators in Dublin by raiding Liberty Hall, the headquarters of the IGTWU, which was known to be a hotbed of sedition.

However, in the mistaken belief that the building was heavily fortified, a proviso was made that any operation would be postponed until a field gun could be dispatched from Athlone.

The following day, with Dublin in a festive mood to celebrate the Easter Bank Holiday, the authorities were taken completely by surprise as columns of Volunteers seized a number of strategic buildings throughout the city. Taken unawares, Irish Command could only attempt to stabilize the situation until the extent of the insurrection became known and accordingly the adjutant, Colonel H. V. Cowan, immediately called the commanders of the three infantry regiments within the city – the 3rd Royal Irish Rifles, the 3rd Royal Irish Regiment and the 10th Royal Dublin Fusiliers – and instructed them to send their outlying pickets to Dublin Castle, firstly to protect the civil administration, and secondly to have some form of consolidated military presence within the city.

Cowan's next call was to Brigadier W. H. M. Lowe at the Curragh requesting that the elements of the 3rd Reserve Cavalry and 25th Reserve Infantry Brigades stationed there be moved to Dublin to assist in putting down the rebellion. Additional calls were then put through to the Reserve Artillery Brigade at Athlone and the 15th Reserve Infantry Brigade at Belfast asking that reinforcements be sent to Dublin post-haste. Finally, at around 1300hrs an officer in mufti made his way to the naval base at Kingstown where he was able to send a wireless message to London outlining the calamitous events of the early afternoon. All that could now be done was to sit and await developments.

# THE BATTLE

## PRELUDE

O n 9 April 1916, the Norwegian steamer *Aud* raised anchor at the German port of Lübeck and headed for sea. At first glance there was nothing remarkable about the ship, but a closer investigation would have revealed that she was in fact a German vessel, the *Libau*, whose appearance had been altered to resemble that of the Norwegian merchantman in order to confuse Allied agents or warships whom she might encounter whilst at sea. This was not, however, the limit of the deception for she was originally an English merchantman interned by Germany at the beginning of the war and converted for service with the Imperial Navy.

Commanded by Kapitänleutnant Karl Spindler, the *Aud*'s mission was to transport some 20,000 captured Russian rifles, 10 machine guns, a million rounds of ammunition and a quantity of explosives to a rendezvous point on the west coast of Ireland where, coordinating its arrival with a submarine carrying members of the Irish Brigade, Roger Casement, Robert Monteith and Daniel Bailey, it was to land the armaments and distribute them to waiting members of the Irish Volunteers.

The plan was simple: protected by a neutral flag, *Aud* would bypass the main British patrol areas by hugging the Norwegian coast and sailing northwards into the Arctic Circle then changing course to head through Denmark Strait. The plan worked surprisingly well with *Aud* being submitted to only the most cursory of inspections by passing British patrol vessels but, as the time came to make the south-western run, concerns about an unseasonable movement in the pack ice persuaded Spindler to make his turn between Iceland and the Faeroes instead.

Boarding the *U-19*, the Irishmen had a relatively incident-free voyage to the west coast of Ireland. Cruising on the surface at night and travelling submerged by day the German submarine followed the course set by *Aud*. Their journey was made marginally worse by Casement's continuing ill health and an injury that Monteith received to his hand in Germany whilst demonstrating a machine gun to members of the brigade.

The plan was that both vessels would rendezvous in Tralee Bay and, after establishing contact with local Volunteers, unload and distribute the arms. However, given the unpredictability of the weather and chance encounters with Royal Navy vessels the 'time window' had been left relatively vague, something upon which the whole success of the mission would hinge for, unknown to either the *Clann*, the Supreme Council or the Germans, British Naval Intelligence had broken the ciphers used in correspondence between Berlin and the German Embassy in Washington DC and were thus fully aware of the negotiations taking place in America concerning German support for an Irish rebellion.

Flag of the Irish Republic flying from the roof of the GPO. Flying at the corner of Sackville Street and Princes Street, the Republican flag flutters defiantly in the breeze; a position it held until the building was consumed by flames and evacuated on 28 April. (Courtesy National Museum of Ireland, Dublin – HE1195/B273)

On the morning of 20 April, and totally unrelated to either Spindler's or Weissbach's missions, another German submarine, the *U-69*, shelled the British steamer *Cairngowan* some 55 miles west of Fastnet Rock and as British patrol sloops moved to intercept the intruder they opened a gap in the picket line into which both vessels sailed, oblivious of their good fortune, en route for Tralee.

By mid-afternoon *Aud* was approaching the Irish coast but missed the rendezvous point and hove to overnight off the Magharee Islands. At dawn the following day, a patrol sloop, the *Setter II*, came alongside, but her commander was so completely taken in by her disguise that he failed to take any further action.

Meanwhile, the *U-19* had surfaced and, failing to contact the *Aud*, Weissbach decided to land his passengers on a local beach, the Banna Strand. Disembarkation was difficult – the sea rough and the German captain unwilling to remain on the surface longer than was absolutely necessary. With Casement having been ill for the duration of the voyage, Bailey and the injured Monteith had to manfully guide a collapsible boat to shore, narrowly escaping drowning a scant few yards from their destination. It was clear that Casement was in no condition to continue and so, after burying the boat and their personal weapons in the sand, they left their companion in the shelter of a local ruin and moved inland to meet their contacts.

It was not long before Casement was discovered and, after attempting to bluff his way out of capture, it was soon apparent to the authorities that this was in fact the attempt to land German arms for the Irish Volunteers. Another vessel, the armed trawler *Lord Heneage*, was then sent to question the *Aud*'s captain further and, shortly after 1300hrs on 21 April, Spindler ordered the ship's anchor raised and he headed out to sea in an attempt to escape the British warship. Here the advantage of the British patrol system became apparent as *Setter II* now joined in the chase, whilst by late afternoon the patrol sloops *Zinnia* and *Bluebell*, returned on station from their fruitless pursuit of the *U-69*, effectively encircling the 'Norwegian' ship and preventing her escape.

**33**

The small flotilla continued south-westwards and the following morning orders were received for *Aud* to be brought into Queenstown where she would be boarded and searched. Escorted now only by the *Bluebell* Spindler outwardly complied but ordered his crew to change into their naval uniforms and prepare to abandon ship. At a little after 0920hrs on 22 April, the battle ensign of the Imperial German Navy broke out on the *Aud*'s flagstaff, and a few minutes later a series of dull thuds signalled the explosion of the charges that sent the ship and her cargo to the bottom, just outside the port.

Although on a qualitative par with the majority of the Howth Mausers, the weapons carried by the *Aud* would not have secured victory for the Rebels, but they would most certainly have prolonged the fighting. Their loss would be crucially felt in the coming week.

## LAST-MINUTE CHANGES

Their plans made, the putative Rebels began their final preparations in earnest. With the addition of James Connolly to their ranks, drill was supplemented with courses on such diverse subjects as street fighting, urban fortifications and the manufacture of explosives.

At Liberty Hall, Battalion HQs and 'safe houses' throughout the city, stores of food and rudimentary medical supplies were laid down against the day when the order to rise was to be given.

In January 1916, Pearse had issued an order to all Volunteers, warning them to prepare for a series of special manoeuvres to take place during Easter Week and, as a result, an alarmed Éoin MacNeill challenged his subordinate about whether he was planning insurrection.

The glib reply was that he was not, and the matter was left there, only to be resurrected on St Patrick's Day when the Nationalists held a number of rallies in Dublin, culminating in a large section of the city centre being cordoned off by armed Volunteers whilst their compatriots passed in review before their chief of staff.

For the moderates, it was another demonstration of why the British Government, the Redmondite National Volunteers and indeed the

Damage to the exterior of the Royal College of Surgeons, St Stephen's Green. As Mallin's men were forced away from St Stephen's Green they retreated into the College of Surgeons, which was raked by machine-gun fire from the upper floors of the Shelbourne Hotel. (Courtesy Imperial War Museum, London – HU55525)

Ulster Unionists should ignore the Irish Volunteers at their peril; but for the members of the Supreme Council and their adherents it was yet another vindication of their course, for the authorities had neither interfered with the review nor with a number of dummy attacks that had been staged on various important buildings within the city. All was now ready for Pearse's 'special manoeuvres'.

As March ended and April began, preparations in Ireland and Germany continued apace, but there was a potentially fatal flaw in the IRB's planning. When Bulmer Hobson had been ousted from the inner circle of the Supreme Council, he had remained Secretary to the Irish Volunteers and thus retained considerable influence within the movement. It was to him therefore that two senior Volunteer officers – J. J. 'Ginger' O'Connell and Eimar O'Duffy – turned late on the evening of Thursday 20 April with the news that a number of the provincial companies had been ordered to prepare for a Rising to take place on Easter Sunday. Shocked, but not surprised by the revelation, Hobson immediately drove the two men to see MacNeill who listened aghast to their report and then demanded that all three accompany him to challenge Pearse over the allegations.

'I've just learned that you've issued orders for an Insurrection!' MacNeill stormed as he was shown into Pearse's study in the early hours of Good Friday morning. Pearse saw no point in denying the accusation as the tirade continued, 'I'll not be responsible for the calling out of a half-armed force, and I'll do anything needed to prevent an unnecessary waste of lives, anything – that is – short of calling up Dublin Castle!' Believing the affair nipped in the bud, they left, but Pearse made the irrevocable decision that the planned Rising would still go ahead and prepared to meet with the other members of the Supreme Council to warn them of his meeting with the incensed chief of staff.

Pearse met first with MacDermott and MacDonagh, and it was decided that the three of them would make a final attempt to dissuade MacNeill from his attempts to sabotage their plans.

His anger still simmering, the chief of staff refused to have anything to do with either of the two academics and would only talk to

MacDermott who, ushered into MacNeill's bedroom, saw no point in dissembling – a significant cargo of German arms was to be landed in Kerry during the course of the day, but he was met by a solid reiteration of the intent to forestall any attempt to incite rebellion. MacDermott then changed tack and handed MacNeill the bitter pill of betrayal, confirming the solid layer of IRB supporters who stood between him and the Volunteer rank and file, emphasizing the fact that the German arms would ensure conflict with the British authorities and leaving the nationalists with two simple choices. Bowed by the stark reality of MacDermott's revelation, MacNeill wearily answered, 'If it's a choice of fighting or being suppressed, then I shall fight'. With this seeming concession in their hands, the three IRB men then prepared to tell their fellow conspirators of the defused situation.

Good Friday saw two events that once more threw the Supreme Council's plans into a state of confusion. The first was the news of Casement's capture and the scuttling of the *Aud*, whilst the second was a problem entirely of their own making: in an attempt to further isolate MacNeill from his moderate advisers, the Council had arranged for Bulmer Hobson to be kidnapped and taken to a safe house where he was to be held until the end of the Rising. This lead to Michael O'Rahilly, the Volunteers' Treasurer who was more commonly known as 'the O'Rahilly', bursting into Pearse's study brandishing a loaded pistol and shouting 'whoever you send for me, make sure that he's quick on the trigger!' Eventually he calmed down and tried to persuade his colleague to change his plans but, seeing that he could not influence Pearse, left as suddenly as he had come intending to raise the matter with MacNeill.

News of the Kerry debacle had only served to restore the chief of staff's confidence and so, on Easter Saturday, he travelled once more to Pearse's where, after an extremely acrimonious exchange, he declared that he would forbid the Volunteers from taking part in any military exercises on the following day, and gave the conspirators a few hours in which to change their minds and abort what he perceived as arrant folly. No subsequent communication was received from either Pearse or the others and so, shortly after 2200hrs, couriers were sent to the various provincial brigade commanders: 'Volunteers completely deceived. All orders for special action are hereby cancelled – on no account will action be taken'. A 'Gaelic Paul Revere', the O'Rahilly travelled by taxi to Cork, Kerry, Tipperary and Limerick to deliver the chief of staff's instructions before returning, exhausted, in the early hours of Easter Saturday evening, confident that disaster had been averted.

As the messengers left, MacNeill sat down to play his final card – an open announcement that he intended to have published in the *Dublin Sunday Independent* as a direct appeal to the Volunteers' rank and file:

> *Owing to the critical position, all orders given to Irish Volunteers*
> *for tomorrow, Easter Sunday, are hereby rescinded and no parades,*
> *marches or other movements of the Irish Volunteers will take place.*
> *Each individual Volunteer will obey this order strictly in every particular.*

To ensure publication, MacNeill himself delivered it by hand to the newspaper's editor. Many have come to believe that this announcement was the single main cause of the low turn-out of Volunteers 24 hours later

As the morning of Easter Sunday 1916 dawned, large numbers of Volunteers were in the process of attending Holy Mass, but at Liberty Hall, the Citizen Army HQ, the attention of the IRB Supreme Council was firmly focused on the *Dublin Sunday Independent*. Incredulous, they were forced to admit that a man whom they had deceived for so long had outmanoeuvred them.

The only question was therefore how to react – Clarke advocated that the Rising go ahead as planned, on the premise that once the firing had started Volunteers throughout the country would join in irrespective of the announcement in the newspaper. Pearse and MacDermott disagreed, arguing that although the damage had been done the situation was not irretrievable, and that they simply needed to redraw their immediate plans in light of the new situation. Thus when Connolly cast his deciding vote in favour of a postponement until midday on Easter Monday, there were no voices of dissent.

# MONDAY 24 APRIL – A CITY TAKEN UNAWARES

Easter Monday 1916 saw Dublin in festive mood. The weather was unseasonably warm and many had taken advantage of the holiday period to take in the horse racing at Fairyhouse.

Despite the considerable interest in the 'sport of kings', Dublin still played host to a large number of holidaymakers, many of whom were British soldiers on leave from their units and who would, inevitably, be caught up in events as they unfolded.

On the morning of 24 April, the British garrison of Dublin numbered a little over 2,400 officers and men, deployed across four of the city's barracks as follows: a short distance from Army HQ at Parkgate, the Marlborough Barracks held some 886 members of the 6th Reserve Cavalry Regiment whilst the nearby Royal Barracks was the depot for 467 officers and men of the 10th Royal Dublin Fusiliers. The Richmond Barracks near the western suburb of Kilmainham was home to 403 men of the 3rd Royal Irish Regiment whilst, completing the garrison were the 671 troops of the 3rd Royal Irish Rifles at the Portobello Barracks, just south of the Grand Canal. Furthermore small pickets were distributed across Dublin, mounting guard on buildings such as the General Post Office in Sackville Street, the Magazine Fort in Phoenix Park and the military warehouses at the North Wall Docks. In addition to the previously mentioned units, some quasi-military units were also available – The Officer Training Corps had cadres at Trinity College and the Royal College of Surgeons and, in addition, a body of veterans known as the 'Georgius Rex' or, more colloquially, the 'Gorgeous Wrecks' were also available. Thus, the main British strength lay to the west of the city, well away from the areas in which the Irish Volunteers and members of the Citizen Army were planning to assemble.

Against this backdrop, the sole military manoeuvres planned on the day were the 'Georgius Rex', who were on a route march in the hills south of Dublin, and a troop of the 6th Reserve Cavalry Regiment, under the command of 2nd Lieutenant G. J. Hunter, who had been sent

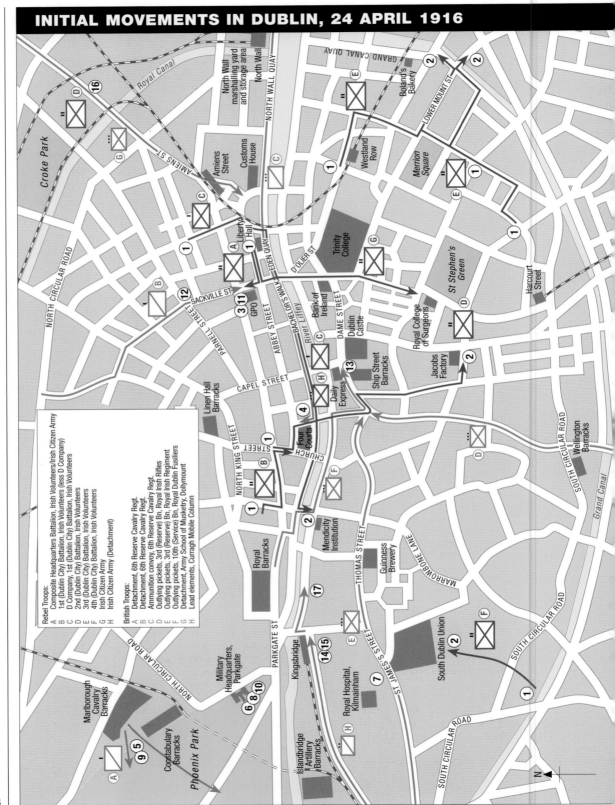

Rebel Troops:
A — Composite Headquarters Battalion, Irish Volunteers/Irish Citizen Army
B — 1st (Dublin City) Battalion, Irish Volunteers (less D Company)
D Company, 1st (Dublin City) Battalion, Irish Volunteers
C — 2nd (Dublin City) Battalion, Irish Volunteers
D — 3rd (Dublin City) Battalion, Irish Volunteers
E — 3rd (Dublin City) Battalion, Irish Volunteers
F — 4th (Dublin City) Battalion, Irish Volunteers
G — Irish Citizen Army
H — Irish Citizen Army (Detachment)

British Troops:
A — Detachment, 6th Reserve Cavalry Regt.
B — Detachment, 6th Reserve Cavalry Regt.
C — Ammunition convoy, 6th Reserve Cavalry Regt.
D — Outlying pickets, 3rd (Reserve) Bn, Royal Irish Rifles
E — Outlying pickets, 3rd (Reserve) Bn, Royal Irish Regiment
F — Outlying pickets, 10th (Service) Bn, Royal Dublin Fusiliers
G — Detachment, Army School of Musketry, Dollymount
H — Lead elements, Curragh Mobile Column

to the North Wall Docks with orders to escort an ammunition convoy through the city to the Magazine Fort in Phoenix Park, a particularly humdrum assignment for a Bank Holiday Monday.

They were not, however, the only ones active that morning. In response to MacDonagh's instructions, the Dublin City Brigade's four battalion commanders had been issuing a repeat of the previous day's mobilization orders to their men by courier, word of mouth, whatever means came to hand.

With the Volunteer battalions raised geographically, the north-west of the city was represented by the 1st Battalion under the command of Edward 'Ned' Daly who, at 25, was the youngest of the Volunteer commandants but the one with the most impeccable credentials. The scion of a long established Republican family, he was also the brother-in-law of Thomas Clarke. The majority of the battalion concentrated around Blackhall Street, where some 250 men eventually assembled for duty, the exception being the dozen or so men of D Company, led by Captain Seán Heuston, who formed at Mountjoy Square and would later be acting under the direct orders of James Connolly.

Daly's task would be to occupy and fortify an area of the city centred around the Four Courts complex on King's Inn Quay, extending his lines north towards Phibsboro, and guarding against attacks coming in from the west of Dublin, primarily from British troops moving from both the Marlborough and Royal Barracks.

The north-east of Dublin was the recruiting ground for MacDonagh's own 2nd Battalion and here all was confusion. The men had been originally due to muster at Father Matthew Park in Fairview, but this was changed at the last minute to a location near St Stephen's Green, thereby resulting in the unit being split with roughly 200 or so men following the new instructions. A number of men who turned up in Fairview after the Rising had started were directed to the GPO in Sackville Street to reinforce the garrison there rather than to follow the main body in occupying the Jacobs Biscuit Factory in Bishop Street.

1.  1000hrs: Rebel forces begin to assemble at muster points throughout Dublin.
2.  1130hrs: Rebel forces move to secure strategic targets within city, and establish outlying defensive positions.
3.  1155hrs: Rebel Headquarters Battalion seizes the General Post Office.
4.  1200hrs: British Ammunition Convoy is ambushed near the Four Courts building.
5.  1217hrs: Rebels attack the Magazine Fort in Phoenix Park but fail to secure munitions stored there.
6.  1210hrs: Colonel Cowan orders the 6th Reserve Cavalry to send a patrol to Sackville Street and for the three battalions of the Dublin Garrison to send their pickets to defend Dublin Castle.
7.  1220hrs: A picket of the 3rd Royal Irish Regt. comes under fire from South Dublin Union. Twenty men sent forward to Dublin Castle whilst the remainder await the balance of the regiment to arrive.
8.  1230hrs: Colonel Cowan reaches the Curragh by telephone and requests that the mobile column of the 3rd Reserve Cavalry Bde. is sent to Dublin.
9.  1230hrs: Wimborne orders the 6th Reserve Cavalry to send detachments to defend the Magazine Fort and the Viceregal Lodge in Phoenix Park.
10. 1235hrs: Colonel Cowan calls for additional rein forcements from other British bases.
11. 1245hrs: Patrick Pearse proclaims the establishment of the Irish Republic from the entrance to the GPO.
12. 1240hrs: A troop of the 6th Reserve Cavalry Regt. proceeds down Sackville St and is engaged by Rebel forces occupying the GPO and buildings opposite.
13. 1340hrs: Pickets of the 3rd Royal Irish Rifles and 10th Royal Dublin Fusiliers arrive at the Ship Street Barracks after coming under fire from the Jacobs Factory and Mendicity Institution respectively.
14. 1600hrs: Lead elements of the Curragh Mobile Column arrive and secure Kingsbridge Railway Station.
15. 1625hrs: Trains carrying the main body of troops from the Curragh begin to arrive at Kingsbridge Station at 15–20 minute intervals.
16. 1630hrs: A detachment from the Army Musketry School at Dollymount filters through the city to secure the facilities at North Wall.
17. 1730hrs: The Curragh Mobile Column begins to drive along the Quays toward Dublin Castle.

The Upper Gate of Dublin Castle. From here, the British launched a series of attacks that eventually forced their way into the enemy-held City Hall, paving the way for the consolidation of the castle area. (Courtesy David Murphy)

In the south-east, the 34-year-old American-born schoolteacher, Eamon de Valera, commanding the 3rd Battalion, was having as little luck with the mobilization orders as his fellow battalion commanders. Only 130 men fell in at the muster points in Brunswick Street, Earlsfort Terrace and Oakley Road, a pale shadow of the anticipated turn-out especially in view of the fact that the 3rd Battalion was deputed to neutralize the British forces occupying the Beggars Bush Barracks in Cranmer Street as well as blocking the advance of any reinforcements moving on Dublin from the naval base at Kingstown.

The 4th City Battalion had arguably been given the hardest task of all – to defend against the inevitable British counterattack that was expected to come from the base at the Curragh in Co. Kildare, some 30 miles south-west of Dublin. Commanded by Eamonn Céannt, probably the most aggressively minded of the four battalion commanders, the unit mustered in the south-western suburb of Dolphin's Barn and was probably the hardest hit by the reduced turn-out of Volunteers, mustering a mere 100 men to occupy the largest of the four battalion areas which, centred on the South Dublin Union, covered the area to the south of Kilmainham.

At about 1000hrs[1] those Volunteers who had received their changes of orders began to congregate at their various muster points. These ranged from men in full uniform to those whose sole acquiescence to such regulations lay in the ammunition bandoliers they wore draped over their shoulders or a yellow armband denoting their Volunteer membership; from those who carried modern rifles and shotguns to those who bore antique firearms or even home-made pikes, which would have seemed more in place in 1798 than in 1916. As their numbers increased, and under the watchful eyes of the battalion commandants, company officers moved up and down the ranks, taking the rolls and issuing initial instructions.

The Bedford Tower and Upper Castle Yard of Dublin Castle. From this vantage point, British snipers were able to engage and dominate targets in Dame Street and the surrounding areas, providing valuable support for the attacks on City Hall and the Express Building. (Courtesy David Murphy)

---

1 At the time of the Easter Rising, Ireland ran on Dublin Mean Time, which was approximately 25 minutes behind Greenwich Mean Time. For continuity, all timings have been given as GMT – DMT was abolished on 23 August 1916.

British forces outside City Hall. Following the capture of Dublin's City Hall and the adjacent enemy positions, British forces are seen erecting barbed-wire defences to impede an expected counter-attack by Rebel forces. (Courtesy National Museum of Ireland, Dublin – HE1172/B273)

One such body was the so-called 'Kimmage Garrison', a body of expatriate Irishmen who had been smuggled some time earlier into the grounds of the Plunkett family estate where they had been undergoing training. Commanded by Captain George Plunkett, they made their way into the south-west of the city, making a stylish entrance into the Rising when Plunkett stopped a tram at gunpoint and, as his heavily armed men boarded the vehicle, holstered his pistol and opening his wallet turned to the driver with the immortal words 'Fifty-Two tuppenny tickets to the City Centre please'.

Whilst these preparations were going on, the Supreme Council – with the exception of MacDonagh – gathered together. Now constituting the Provisional Government of the Irish Republic their task was to secure the General Post Office building in Sackville Street and from there, Patrick Pearse, President of the said Republic would proclaim its establishment to the world.

At a little after 1140hrs the 'Fall In' was sounded outside Liberty Hall and within minutes the street was crowded as almost 400 members of the Volunteers, Citizen Army and other Republican organizations began to assemble. For the first time in over a century armed men stood in Dublin's streets with the intention of overthrowing the British Government.

Stocky and bow-legged, Connolly strode over to Michael Mallin, his deputy and now de facto field commander of the Citizen Army, ordering him to take a group of 100 or so and occupy St Stephen's Green, acting not only as a vital link between the 2nd and 3rd Battalions, but also to control a position from which pressure could be put on both Dublin Castle and Trinity College. In turn, Mallin was assisted by one of the more colourful members of the Volunteer Movement – the Countess Constance Markiewicz, an Anglo-Irish aristocrat who having married a Polish Count had wholeheartedly embraced the Republican cause. Resplendent in her immaculately tailored uniform, she brandished an oversize pistol to encourage the men as they moved off.

## THE 'LANCERS' IN SACKVILLE STREET, 24 APRIL 1916.
(Pages 42–43)

Almost as soon as they had occupied the General Post Office, the Rebels began to fortify the building using whatever materials came to hand – furniture, postal sacks, ledgers – any thing that would serve to block a window or provide a modicum of cover (1). As news of the Rising spread, a detachment of the 6th Reserve Cavalry Regiment, under Col. Hammond, was sent from the Marlborough Barracks, near Phoenix Park, to investigate and report upon the situation in Sackville Street. Unsure of the situation, Hammond halted his command at the Parnell Memorial at the northern end of Sackville Street, and sent forward a small patrol to secure the information required. As the troopers passed the Nelson Pillar, many of the insurgents within the Post Office abandoned their attempts at building breastworks and armed with an eclectic mix of firearms, rushed to the windows to be amongst the first to strike a blow against the enemy (2). On the ground floor of the GPO, James Connolly (3), moved amongst the men encouraging them and cautioning them to await the orders to fire, being joined by Capt. Michael Collins (4), one of Joseph Plunkett's aides, who had come to the front of the building in order to observe and report on developments. As part of a training formation, the cavalrymen (5) included recruits from four units, the 5th and 12th Lancers

and two regiments of London Yeomanry. Contrary to many reports only a number of the men were actually armed with lances. Despite Connolly's exhortations, many of his men – as well as those in the buildings opposite – fired early (6) and the intended crossfire was not as effective as had been hoped with three troopers being killed and a fourth dismounted when his horse was shot from under him. Another British casualty was narrowly averted when a round fired from the positions across from the GPO, splintered the telephone booth in which Lt. Chalmers was being held prisoner. First blood had indeed been struck, but it was a double-edged sword. The British were now painfully aware that Sackville Street was being held in strength by the enemy and, until the situation became clearer, were more inclined to err on the side of caution whilst amongst the GPO garrison – and Connolly especially – there developed a belief that it would only be a matter of time before the British ordered a frontal assault upon the GPO, which would be bloodily repulsed by the defenders. This misconception on Connolly's part persisted throughout the week, only to remain unrealised when the burning building was finally evacuated late on the evening of Friday 28 April, although – ironically – the British had indeed planned to assault the GPO during the Saturday morning, but cancelled their plans when the building was found to be unoccupied.

When Mallin's command reached St Stephen's Green, they immediately started to dig defensive positions within the lawns and bushes and began to construct roadblocks, often using the power of a loaded weapon to ensure compliance. Strangely enough for a man with previous military experience – he had served with the British Army in India – Mallin neglected to take immediate notice of either the Shelbourne Hotel or the Royal College of Surgeons, two buildings that dominated the area. This lapse would have dramatic effects as the fighting spread.

Connolly then sent a small detachment under the command of Captain Seán Connolly to seize the area around City Hall and interdict the movement of British forces attempting to use the main gateway to the castle or the entrance to the Ship Street Barracks. Approaching the castle, they were challenged by Constable James O'Brien of the Dublin Metropolitan Police who was shot and killed by Connolly as the party attempted to rush the gates. The guardhouse was also overrun but the Rebels were cheated of an inestimable prize when the few soldiers within the castle rallied, closing the gates to the upper and lower yards before either Connolly or his men could react further.

A party of Volunteers acting the part of amateur footballers, 'lost' their ball at the entrance to the Magazine Fort in Phoenix Park and over-powered the guards with the intent of destroying the facility and stealing quantities of explosives for use by the Rebel forces. They were thwarted, however, by the fact that the officer of the day had absented himself to the Fairyhouse Races and had taken the keys to the magazine with him. One of the many tragedies of the Rising was soon to be played out however, as amongst the prisoners were the family of the fort's commandant. As civilians, they were set free on the condition that they did not attempt to give a warning of what had just happened but, as they dispersed, one of the family's teenage sons bolted for some nearby houses, pursued by Volunteer Gary Holohan. The young man was beating on a door just as Holohan caught and shot him. Moments later, the charges that had been

This memorial is dedicated to Captain Seán Connolly and members of the Citizen Army who were killed in the defence of City Hall by British counter-attacks from Dublin Castle. (Author's collection)

British cavalry on patrol in Sackville Street, May 1916. Although taken after the Rising, this image gives a perfect description of the composition of a unit of the cavalry reserve. All patrol members are armed and equipped as per their parent units – lancers, yeomanry, etc. The fact that these troopers are indeed mounted would suggest that they are members of the 6th Reserve Cavalry Regiment, the only such unit to retain their horses during the fighting. (Courtesy Corbis Images)

set in the fort detonated, giving the warning that Holohan had sought to avoid.

Back at Liberty Hall, Connolly was busily marshalling the rest of his forces into formation, joined at the head of the column by Pearse and Plunkett. Just as the order to move off was about to be given, a motor car laden with arms and ammunition turned the corner and pulled up alongside the troops. Aboard was 'the O'Rahilly' who, with characteristic good grace, was prepared to forget his opposition to the Rising now that it had become a reality – 'having helped to wind the clock, it would be a shame not to hear it chime!' About ten minutes before midday, the column moved off towards Sackville Street. Observed by British officers in the Metropole Hotel, the formation halted under Connolly's orders in front of the GPO Building and the following order was issued: 'Battalion halt! Battalion, left face! The GPO Building – CHARGE!'

The men rushed into the building and began to herd the occupants – whether employees or customers – into the public hall and, as they arrived, others began the process of securing the building and preparing it for defence. One such party headed up to the telegraph room and came face to face with a group of British soldiers on guard duty; before the troops could react, one of the Volunteers fired his pistol and wounded the sergeant in command. At this point the troops surrendered after lowering their unloaded rifles and allowed their NCO to be taken away for treatment. Another accidental captive was 2nd Lieutenant A. D. Chalmers of the 14th Royal Fusiliers who was captured in the act of sending a postcard to his wife. With no facilities as yet organized for the holding of prisoners, Chalmers was trussed up with telephone cable and left in one of the public phone booths. For the next hour or so, the entire building was a scene of organized chaos as the Volunteers attempted to fortify their position, under the watchful eyes of Connolly and Captain W. J. Brennan-Whitmore, one of Joseph Plunkett's aides.

As these events unfolded, Lt. Hunter led his men at a slow trot from North Wall, heading along the quays parallel to the Liffey. Unknown to the cavalryman was the fact that his entire route was under observation by parties of Volunteers manning outlying positions to cover the GPO area. With strict orders to hold their fire, the irregulars allowed the convoy to pass. All changed however, when the small column passed in front of the Four Courts. A group of men were building a barricade on the corner of Church Street and, seeing the British soldiers, grabbed their weapons and fired off a loose volley. Several men were hit including Hunter, who was mortally wounded, and the formation scattered with the majority finding themselves in Charles Street near Ormonde Market. Dismounting, they broke into the Collier Dispensary and the Medical Mission opposite, and began to fortify their position, bringing the bulk of the arms and ammunition into the buildings.

The explosion at the Magazine Fort and the small-arms fire outside Dublin Castle should have galvanized the Government forces into action but Colonel Kennard, the senior officer in Dublin, was unaccounted for and precious minutes were lost in trying to locate him. Assuming command, the adjutant, Col. Cowan, immediately telephoned the Portobello, Richmond and Royal Barracks to advise the battalion commanders there about the state of emergency and instructed them to send their ready units – approximately 100 men per battalion – to Dublin

Castle to assist in its defence pending the full mobilization of the city garrison. Another hurried call was made to Colonel Hammond at the Marlborough Barracks asking for troops to be sent to Sackville Street to investigate the situation there. After Cowan hung up, Hammond decided to take personal command of the patrol and left at the head of at least two full troops of cavalry for the junction of Parnell and Sackville streets.

Next, Cowan placed a call to the headquarters of Central Command at the Curragh Camp and apprised Brig. W. H. M. Lowe, commander of the 3rd Reserve Cavalry Brigade, of the situation. Lowe immediately ordered the remaining three regiments of his brigade to entrain for Dublin without delay, (the 6th was already in the city). Several further telephone calls were made and soon reinforcements were being mustered in Athlone, Belfast and Templemore – it is also possible that, at this time, the Army Musketry School at Dollymount in north-western Dublin was alerted about the situation as a Major H. F. Somerville was soon en route for the city at the head of a combined body of instructors and trainees. Finally, the only thing remaining was to alert the War Office in London, and an officer wearing mufti cycled to the Naval Base at Kingstown to transmit the message from the wireless station there, which he reached at 1310hrs.

By now, crowds had started to gather outside the GPO and when Pearse stood at the entrance to the building and announced the establishment of an Irish Republic, he was greeted by a stony indifference. Shortly afterwards Hammond's troopers appeared at the top of Sackville Street, and many of the onlookers cheered, waiting to see what short work the Army would make of the insurgents. A small knot of horsemen detached itself from the main body and began to walk down the centre of the road heading towards the Liffey. On both sides of the street, men either crouched behind their improvised breastworks or hung back in the shadows. Connolly, standing by one of the lower windows in the GPO, whispered to the men nearby, exhorting them to keep calm, hold their fire and wait for their targets to present themselves. Onward came the horses and, as they drew level with the GPO, a shot rang out, quickly followed by another and another until finally a ragged volley broke the silence.

As the cavalrymen approached, a group of men were waiting in one of the side streets opposite the post office, they were the men of the Rathfarnham Company of Volunteers who – falling outside of the formal battalion organization – had come to join the Headquarters Battalion. As the British troopers advanced they chose that moment to sprint across Sackville Street, gathering beneath the windows on the southern façade in an attempt to gain entrance to the building. The rifle fire that checked the British probe undoubtedly saved a number of lives and the company was a welcome addition to the GPO garrison.

Despite the obvious disadvantage of their being caught in a crossfire, British casualties were absurdly light – only four troopers were hit, three of whom were killed outright and the last fatally wounded. A fifth British casualty was narrowly avoided when a spent bullet fired from opposite the GPO hit the telephone booth in which Lt. Chalmers lay. The scouting party hurriedly withdrew to the main body and Hammond pulled his troops back to barracks, both to report the incident and await further instructions, whilst amid the inevitable cheers Connolly returned to the business in hand and began to send out requisitioning parties to secure supplies from neighbouring shops and hotels, many of which were by now becoming the target of civilian looters. As an unarmed force, the Dublin Metropolitan Police was withdrawn shortly after the firing started and thus, despite the Volunteers' best intentions, there was little that could be done to check this outbreak of lawlessness. The Dublin Fire Brigade, although able to contain initial spontaneous examples of arson, was also soon withdrawn for the same reasons, with calamitous consequences.

Although it was the farthest away from its objective, the picket from the 3rd Royal Irish Regiment was the first into action. As the troops approached the Mount Brown area they could see outposts manned by men of Céannt's 4th Battalion, and so a detachment of 20 men under Lieutenant George Malone was detailed to continue to Dublin Castle and spring any ambush whilst the remainder of the force took up defensive positions in support. As per standing orders, the men advanced with rifles sloped and unloaded but soon came under point-blank fire from a group of Volunteers under Section-Commander John Joyce. A number of soldiers were killed instantaneously and – unable to return fire – the remainder attempted to force their way into some buildings opposite the rebel positions, with Malone being hit and his jaw shattered as he attempted to drag one of his dying men into cover.

It was clear that the picket was insufficient to force a passage past the 4th Battalion's positions and so the battalion commander, Lieutenant-Colonel Owens, brought up the rest of his command from the Richmond Barracks. A company supported by a Lewis gun was deployed in the nearby Kilmainham Hospital with orders to lay down covering fire whilst the remainder of the battalion under the command of Major Milner was to move along O'Connell Road and enter the South Dublin Union from its southern side. Dividing his force into three main bodies (the others were commanded by Captain Warmington and Lieutenant Ramsay), Milner prepared for action, the signal for the attack coming at 1255hrs when the company in Kilmainham Hospital opened fire. The Irish troops pushed their attack with vigour and Ramsay – a veteran of Gallipoli – was mortally wounded whilst leading an assault on the entrance to the Union. A short truce allowed the British to retrieve their dead and wounded and, as hostilities resumed, Capt. Warmington led another attack on the gateway but was killed almost immediately and his men broke under the intense fire coming from Céannt's positions. A second ceasefire was then permitted to give the British the opportunity to retrieve the casualties suffered during this second, failed attack.

Attempts were made to move eastwards and thus outflank the rebels, but here the Volunteers' deployment initially paid dividends with the infiltrators being enfiladed from the Jameson's Distillery in Marrowbone Lane. Numbers and superior firepower eventually told, and there was nothing that Céannt could do to prevent his outer defences from being breached by the grinding attacks that continued all that afternoon finally securing lodgements in the Women's Infirmary and Wards 16/17 of the Union by 1730hrs.

The fate of the 10th Royal Dublin Fusiliers was much the same as that of their comrades, and, as they prepared to cross the Liffey by the Queen Street Bridge, they came under intense but inaccurate fire from both the Guinness Brewery and the Mendicity Institution, and, with a few losses,

130 men were able to make their way towards Dublin Castle at about 1345hrs, whilst from the Portobello Barracks a detachment of 50 men had, after clearing their way with a trolley-drawn maxim gun, been able to make their way past MacDonagh's positions around the Jacobs Biscuit Factory and enter the castle via the Ship Street entrance. For the time being, at least, it looked as if the seat of government was safe.

As the sporadic fighting continued around the South Dublin Union, the first reinforcements began to reach Dublin. Although a column under Maj. Somerville of the Musketry School at Dollymount was able to press through into the city and secure the rail terminus and dockyard facilities at North Wall, an attempt by a second group of soldiers from the school to take the Amiens Street Station was beaten back by a detachment of McDonagh's 2nd Battalion under the command of Captain Thomas Weafer, who then moved to the GPO to reinforce the garrison there. At 1600hrs, the 'Georgius Rex' returning from their route march were heading towards the Beggars Bush Barracks in two columns when, as the second group approached Northumberland Road, they came under heavy fire from outposts of de Valera's 3rd Battalion.

Many were killed but the remainder of the formation was able to reach safety by scaling the barracks' walls. When word reached him of the killings, Pearse immediately tried to defuse the moral backlash by ordering the Volunteers not to fire on unarmed men, whether in uniform or not, but the damage had been done, despite the fact that as soon as they were armed, the 'GRs' effectively joined the British Garrison as would indeed have been the case in any eventuality.

At the same time, the leading elements of the Curragh Mobile Column under Colonel Portal, alighted at Kingsbridge Station near Kilmainham and, over the next 90 minutes, the 1,500 dismounted troopers arrived at the rail terminus. After assembling some handcarts to transport ammunition and supplies, Portal's first act was to send the 400 or so men of the 8th Reserve Cavalry Regiment by the loop line railway to bolster the defences at North Wall and, covered by a large number of troops in open order, he led the remainder of the column to Dublin Castle. Moving initially along the quays and past the Guinness Brewery the men then filtered through the side streets without meeting serious opposition, eventually reaching the castle at around 1730hrs.

The final British position south of the Liffey at Trinity College had at first seemed ripe for capture by the Volunteers, but as they had seemingly ignored the building complex – possibly because of a perceived lack of numbers – the temporary commander of the OTC was able to increase the garrison to almost 50 men by 1700hrs by arming many of the students and co-opting a number of servicemen on leave and, with the arrival of two regiments of dismounted cavalry within supporting distance at Dublin Castle, the chances of the Rebels seizing the college simply evaporated.

The arrival of the cavalrymen at Dublin Castle had not only stabilized the situation, but had also altered the balance of forces considerably; the British could now count on something in the region of 4,500 officers and men, whilst the Volunteers – even with the addition of late arrivals – could probably only muster a quarter of the number. The question was now how best to proceed?

The nearest Rebel position to the castle was the City Hall, which had been occupied by Seán Connolly's men since their failed attempt to rush

**1916 Memorial, Mount Street Canal Bridge. Sited at the southern end of the bridge, this pillar marks the bloodiest combat of the Easter Rising. (Author's collection)**

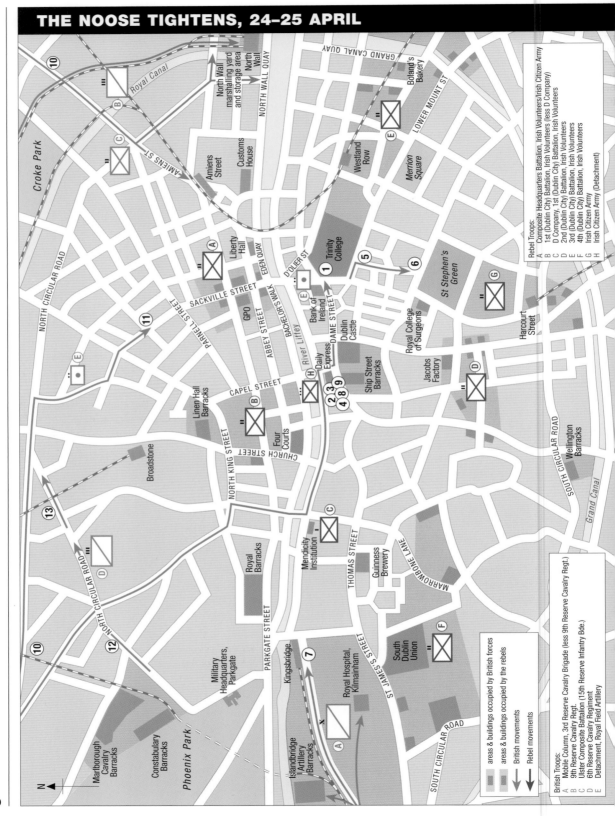

**Rebel Troops:**
A   Composite Headquarters Battalion, Irish Volunteers/Irish Citizen Army
B   1st (Dublin City) Battalion, Irish Volunteers (less D Company)
C   D Company, 1st (Dublin City) Battalion, Irish Volunteers
D   2nd (Dublin City) Battalion, Irish Volunteers
E   3rd (Dublin City) Battalion, Irish Volunteers
F   4th (Dublin City) Battalion, Irish Volunteers
G   Irish Citizen Army
H   Irish Citizen Army (Detachment)

areas & buildings occupied by British forces
areas & buildings occupied by the rebels

British movements
Rebel movements

**British Troops:**
A   Mobile Column, 3rd Reserve Cavalry Brigade (less 9th Reserve Cavalry Regt.)
B   9th Reserve Cavalry Regt.
C   Ulster Composite Battalion (15th Reserve Infantry Bde.)
D   6th Reserve Cavalry Regiment
E   Detachment, Royal Field Artillery

The New Square, Trinity College, Dublin. During the Rising, this peaceful area was home to a two-gun section of field artillery and ever-increasing numbers of troops as British reinforcements began to reach the city. (Courtesy David Murphy)

the castle gates and from where they had been continually sniping at the castle garrison, with Connolly himself being killed by return fire some time into the afternoon. As evening approached, a composite storming party assembled in the castle yard. A wave of 100 men rushed City Hall and took the Provost Marshal's building, but was unable to penetrate farther because of internal barricades that the insurgents had erected for just such an eventuality. Another wave of attackers was thrown at the building to add impetus to the first, but was halted by enemy fire and forced back when its commanding officer was killed. With the streets now impassable, a third party – this time also armed with bombs – was sent through the castle cellars and, emerging on the far side of City Hall, whilst machine guns from the castle suppressed the enemy riflemen on the roof, broke into the building from behind the defenders' positions.

As it became certain that their position had been turned, the Citizen Army men withdrew to the upper floors of the building and, in the confusion, each of the British forces continued to fire at the dust-

1. **1900hrs:** OTC and porters defending Trinity College reinforced by numbers of British and Colonial servicemen on leave or convalescence in Dublin.
2. **1900hrs:** Capt. Elliotson of the Curragh Mobile Column conducts a reconnaissance of the Rebel position based around the City Hall and Rates Office.
3. **1930hrs:** Dublin Castle Garrison sorties out against City Hall. With machine-gun support the third wave is able to break into the building.
4. **2000hrs:** Interior of City Hall is cleared of Rebels, who still hold the roof.
5. **0215hrs:** Capt. Elliotson and a machine-gun group of 100 men moves off under cover of darkness to secure the Shelbourne Hotel on the north side of St Stephen's Green.
6. **0320hrs:** Elliotson's troops occupy the Shelbourne and adjacent Royal Services Club.
7. **0345hrs:** Brigadier Lowe arrives at Kingsbridge Station with the remainder of 25th Reserve Infantry Brigade, taking personal command of British forces in Dublin.
8. **0600hrs:** Supported by machine guns firing from Dublin Castle, British forces secure the roof of City Hall.
9. **1400hrs:** Dublin Castle Garrison sorties out against Rebel positions in and around the Daily Mail Building. Enemy positions are finally cleared after an hour and several bayonet charges.
10. **1400hrs:** Additional reinforcements begin to arrive: Reserve Artillery from Athlone, 4th Royal Dublin Fusiliers from Templemore and the Ulster Composite Battalion from Belfast.
11. **1500hrs:** An 18-pdr artillery section based in the Grangegorman Asylum opens fire on Rebel positions in the Phibsboro area.
12. **1515hrs:** 6th Reserve Cavalry Regt, throws aggressive patrols out towards Phibsboro.
13. **1630hrs:** With artillery and machine-gun support, 6th Reserve Cavalry secure Rebel positions.

obscured figures to their front, unaware that the enemy had slipped away to relative safety. With night falling, the ground floor of City Hall was occupied by British troops, whilst the remainder of the building was very much in the hands of Rebel forces who spent the night anxiously waiting for the inevitable dawn assault.

With events in Dublin unfolding, Captain Alpin, the Chief Naval Officer at Kingstown, having received a request from Col. Cowan that a Royal Navy vessel be deployed on the Liffey, decided to investigate matters for himself and sailed for Dublin in an armed trawler with a patrol vessel, the *Helga II*, as escort. Although he saw no cause for alarm and returned to Kingstown, Alpin ordered the *Helga II* to remain 'on station' on the Liffey, supported by a second armed trawler, the *Sealark II*, which had been undergoing repairs in the Dublin Docks.

## TUESDAY 25 APRIL – THE NOOSE BEGINS TO TIGHTEN

At 0345hrs in the morning, further trains arrived at Kingsbridge Station, carrying not only additional reinforcements – 5th Leinsters and 5th Royal Dublin Fusiliers – but also Brig. W. H. M. Lowe who became the ranking British officer in Dublin. Lowe was aware that his tenure of command would most likely be of short duration as the previous afternoon Lord French, C.-in-C. Home Forces, had authorized the transfer of the 59th (North Midland) Division to Ireland to assist in the suppression of the Rising, and thus he adopted a methodical, almost simplistic approach to the problem. The Rebel forces on either side of the Liffey would be separated by a wedge of British troops stretching from Kilmainham through to Trinity College and, as more troops became available, pockets of resistance would be surrounded and, depending on individual circumstances, either crushed or left 'to wither on the vine'.

The first stage of the operation had commenced shortly after midnight when a force of 100 men and four machine guns under Captain Carl Elliotson was ordered to occupy the Shelbourne Hotel on the north side of St Stephen's Green. Leaving the castle at 0215hrs, the heavily laden soldiers filtered through the backstreets through to Kildare Street, moving slowly to escape detection by Volunteer sentries, and occupied the Shelbourne and the adjacent United Services Club shortly after 0320hrs. They barricaded the lower windows against attack and deployed the machine guns on the fourth floor of the hotel, which gave them a perfect field of fire across the whole of St Stephen's Green; the troopers then grabbed whatever rest they could before daylight.

Dawn broke that Tuesday morning, heavily punctuated by the short, staccato sound of machine guns in action. From Dublin Castle, the suppressing fire was the signal for the British troops who had spent all night in occupation of the ground floor of City Hall to assault the stairwells and, within a short period of time, the building had been carried with all bar one of the Rebel garrison being either killed or captured.

At St Stephen's Green, Mallin's command was given a rude awakening as the machine guns in the Shelbourne Hotel continually

raked the slit trenches and earthworks that had been hurriedly thrown up the previous afternoon. For three hours the Republican forces endured the fusillade, returning a desultory fire as and when possible, but it was no use – Mallin's omission to occupy the hotel had been a costly mistake and now, if there was to be anything salvaged from the position, there was now no option other than withdrawal. Accordingly a little after 0630hrs word began to filter through the ranks that the command was to pull back to the West Gate and from there make a run for the Royal College of Surgeons on the corner with York Street.

The first group made the short dash unscathed, but the second and subsequent groups had to run the gauntlet of British fire from the north side of the green. This was not the only danger as three Citizen Army men from one of the outlying positions were chased up to the college by a mob of irate civilians hurling abuse and rotten vegetables! From a defensive point of view, Mallin's men were in arguably a better position inside the building rather than outside in the open but it was cold, with an inoperative heating system, and the only real food supply consisted of what the men and women under his command had remembered to gather up before the mad sprint from the green and, as if this were not enough, many of the garrison later complained of the permeating odour of formaldehyde and other medical preservatives.

Throughout the morning, the skirmishing continued around the South Dublin Union, but, unsure of the size of the rebel forces defending the facility and confounded by fire coming from supporting positions, the British contented themselves with simply maintaining contact with the enemy. Had either Lowe or Lt. Col. Owens been aware that the force opposing them had mustered a paltry 100 men the previous day, then the arrival of the 4th Royal Dublin Fusiliers during the early afternoon would no doubt have spurred them into making a more aggressive showing; but this is with the benefit of hindsight, and so Céannt and his men continued to hold off a force almost 20 times their number whilst the 5th Leinsters were pushed forwards to reinforce the garrison of Trinity College.

Although the Republican forces in the east of the city – with the exception of the GPO garrison – had been largely passive, the situation was greatly stabilized with the arrival from Belfast of a composite battalion of 1,000 men drawn from the units of the 15th Reserve Infantry Brigade. Their arrival facilitated the dispatch of an 'armoured train' from Amiens Street Station to repair damage to the railway lines, but as its crew were working on the tracks near Annesley Bridge they came under attack from a detachment of Volunteers and lost several men as prisoners.

Buoyed by the success of the early morning, the troops of the castle garrison continued in their attempts to clear the surrounding buildings and a series of bayonet charges were launched at the Mail & Express Offices a little after 1415hrs, with the troops taking only a few moments to gain entry to the ground floor entrance. Connolly's lessons, however, had been well learned and as subsequent waves of soldiers dashed out of the Upper Castle Yard they found their progress inhibited by their comrades who were making little or no progress against Rebel troops fighting from behind barricades. A fifth wave was thrown at the building and the increasing pressure finally broke the defenders who left 22 of their comrades in the smoking ruins.

Farther to the east, the *Helga II* began her participation in the suppression of the Rising mid-afternoon, with a short and desultory bombardment of Boland's Mills at the behest of Army HQ.

The most urgent reinforcement to arrive on Tuesday was the detachment from the Artillery Depot at Athlone, representing the first guns available to Irish Command for use in the suppression of the Rising. The guns themselves were drawn from the 144th and 145th Field Batteries of the 5th Reserve Artillery Brigade and were in a pretty bad state. According to Lieutenant Gerrard, a British officer originally stationed at Athlone but subsequently caught up in Dublin assisting in the defence of Beggars Bush Barracks, the guns were in such bad repair that they had to be cannibalized for parts in order to send any artillery pieces to Dublin whatsoever. A total of four 18-pdrs could be salvaged to form a composite battery, presumably one section of two guns being drawn from each of the two reserve units.

That the guns themselves were Mk. I QF 18-pdrs is borne out by Gerrard when he states that the only shells available for the guns were 'fixed shrapnel', an anti-personnel round whose use against defensive positions and buildings would be somewhat akin to Napoleonic round-shot. The role of the Athlone Battery was therefore limited by ammunition restrictions: there were no high explosive or incendiary shells available, despite the attestations of many Republican participants in the Rising that they were used.

Upon arrival in Dublin, the battery split up into two sections each of two guns. One deployed initially in the grounds of the Grangegorman Lunatic Asylum, whilst the other moved by a circuitous route, crossing the Liffey to the west of the city, and thence following the line of the British advance to Trinity College.

At 1500hrs the field guns at Grangegorman opened fire on an enemy barricade on the North Circular Road near Phibsboro in conjunction with machine guns previously deployed to cover Broadstone Street Station. Shortly afterwards a substantial dismounted patrol of the 6th Reserve Cavalry was thrown out from the Marlborough Barracks with instructions to flush out any Rebel-held strongpoints and clear the North Circular. At 1545hrs, the troopers came within range of the barricade and were able to provide the local pressure that forced the abandonment of the enemy position. Whilst the machine guns certainly encouraged the Volunteers to keep their heads down, the artillery simply punched holes in the barricade, if anything meshing its constituent parts together rather than causing tangible damage to the structure. By 1630hrs the British carried the position and this signalled the collapse of the Rebel outposts in the north of the city, with the various detachments attempting to disengage and retire on the Headquarters Battalion at the GPO.

**A contemporary photograph showing Sackville Street, looking south against a backdrop of flames, suggesting that it was taken on either 27 or 28 April. The GPO can be seen slightly to the right of the Nelson Pillar. (Courtesy Imperial War Museum, London – Q90443)**

It was as the day's fighting was beginning to lull that a British picket from the Portobello Barracks arrested Frank Sheehy-Skeffington – a journalist renowned in the city for his civil rights activities – on the suspicion of being a rebel sympathizer or 'Shinner' as they were now being known from an abbreviation of the Republican movement *Sinn Féin*.

Despite the fact that the British were unable to charge him legally with anything, Skeffington was held until midnight when a Captain Bowen-Colthurst, who was about to lead a raiding patrol into the streets, demanded that the prisoner be turned over to him both as a hostage and a guide. Once outside of the barracks, he handed Skeffington over to his second in command with the admonition that if it became clear that the raid had gone wrong he was to shoot the prisoner. Bowen-Colthurst then ran amok, firstly killing a teenager named Coade claiming that he was acting under the provisions of martial law that had been enacted that day, and then raiding the wrong address where he took two journalists as additional prisoners, bringing his three victims back to the barracks where they were held under arrest, but never charged.

At 1005hrs the following morning, Bowen-Colthurst ordered the sergeant of the guard to assemble the three prisoners in the guardhouse yard and arrange a firing party. As soon as the squad had assembled, the prisoners were ordered to walk to the wall at the far end of the yard and, as they did so, he rapidly barked out the command 'READY – AIM – FIRE!' and, as the three men fell, shot in the back, he simply turned to walk away. As the bodies were inspected, it was believed that Skeffington was still alive and when the departing officer was asked for further instructions he ordered the firing party to shoot again. This time the bodies remained still.

## THE SHERWOOD FORESTERS

Whilst the fighting was raging in Dublin, the British Government was taking measures for the containment and suppression of the unrest in Ireland. Based in Hertfordshire, the 59th (North Midland) Division was Britain's rapid reaction force: deployed across a series of rail hubs north of London, its purpose was to be the counter-threat to any German invasion. Late on Monday afternoon the divisional commander, Major-General Arthur Sandbach, received orders to entrain immediately two of his three brigades for transfer to Dublin, with the remainder of the division to follow with the least possible delay.

Accordingly, orders were sent out to the 178th Brigade (Colonel Maconchy), which would move first, followed by the 177th Brigade (Brigadier Carleton) as soon as sufficient transport had been assembled.

Similar scenes were enacted at brigade headquarters as had been seen in Dublin earlier that day, but eventually some order was injected into the situation and at 0400hrs the 2/5th and 2/6th Sherwood Foresters departed for Liverpool, being followed by the 2/7th at 0830hrs and the 2/8th at 1000hrs. Awaiting the troops was the packet steamer *Ulster*, which would transport the initial lift of troops to the naval base at Kingstown (eventually several additional transports were made available to transfer the division), the brigade being formed there in the early hours of Wednesday 26 April.

Irish Rebellion, May, 1916.
Sackville Street in ruins.

As soon as he arrived in Liverpool, Maconchy was informed that his troops had moved with minimal ammunition – an estimated average of 50 rounds per man – and that, as they had trained to counter a German invasion, no one had an idea of Dublin and its surrounding area. To resolve the former, he made a terse call to the War Office insisting that a total of 400 rounds per man and 10,000 hand grenades be made available at Kingstown before the brigade left the port; whilst to resolve the latter, members of the headquarters staff were detailed to obtain as many maps of Dublin as possible, the majority of these being torn from hotel guidebooks. The munitions were duly delivered to the Kingstown Docks where the small-arms rounds were found to be Mk. VI .303in. ball rather than the Mk. VII with which the troops had been issued whilst in camp. Although of an identical calibre, the difference in their capabilities would require that the men's service rifles would need to be 'zeroed in' to cater for the new rounds or suffer from a resulting loss of accuracy at long and medium ranges.

One oft-mentioned incident in the transfer of the 178th Brigade that needs clarification is that the battalion Lewis guns were left behind as a result of a clerical error or overzealous embarkation officer. They were indeed left behind, but it was a <u>deliberate</u> action. A full-strength battalion would muster some 1,000 officers and men, which would mean that each of the two brigade columns would have had anything up to 2,000 men, whereas the *Ulster* was only designed to carry 1,400 passengers safely.

A Lewis-gun section was not simply a two-man crew, but a group of 26 soldiers to operate and maintain three such weapons in combat, the unit being rounded off by two horses and an ammunition wagon. Simply put, there was insufficient room on the vessel for the sections, the intention undoubtedly being that they would follow on as soon as adequate transport had been arranged. Indeed, D Company, 2/8th Sherwood Foresters, would also remain behind in Liverpool and not rejoin the brigade until the additional transport capacity had been made available and its parent battalion committed to action.

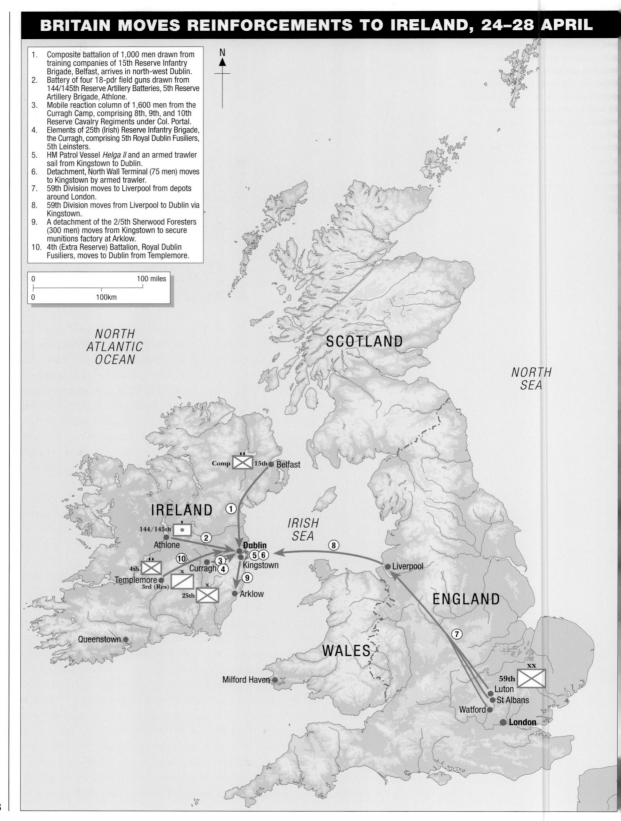

# BRITAIN MOVES REINFORCEMENTS TO IRELAND, 24–28 APRIL

1. Composite battalion of 1,000 men drawn from training companies of 15th Reserve Infantry Brigade, Belfast, arrives in north-west Dublin.
2. Battery of four 18-pdr field guns drawn from 144/145th Reserve Artillery Batteries, 5th Reserve Artillery Brigade, Athlone.
3. Mobile reaction column of 1,600 men from the Curragh Camp, comprising 8th, 9th, and 10th Reserve Cavalry Regiments under Col. Portal.
4. Elements of 25th (Irish) Reserve Infantry Brigade, the Curragh, comprising 5th Royal Dublin Fusiliers, 5th Leinsters.
5. HM Patrol Vessel *Helga II* and an armed trawler sail from Kingstown to Dublin.
6. Detachment, North Wall Terminal (75 men) moves to Kingstown by armed trawler.
7. 59th Division moves to Liverpool from depots around London.
8. 59th Division moves from Liverpool to Dublin via Kingstown.
9. A detachment of the 2/5th Sherwood Foresters (300 men) moves from Kingstown to secure munitions factory at Arklow.
10. 4th (Extra Reserve) Battalion, Royal Dublin Fusiliers, moves to Dublin from Templemore.

An improvised armoured car. As a method of transporting troops and supplies in relative safety a number of vehicles were improvised by bolting boilers from the Guinness Brewery onto the backs of flatbed trucks. In this example a number of rifle/viewing slits have been cut along the sides and hatch of the boiler, with a number of 'dummy' slits painted above and below them in order to confuse enemy marksmen. (Courtesy Imperial War Museum, London – HU73486)

At 0830hrs on the Wednesday morning, Maconchy held a staff meeting in the Kingstown Yacht Club to issue his orders. During the night intelligence had been received from Irish Command that the British forces in Dublin had been taking severe losses and that the direct route into the city was known to be held by the Rebels in strength, covered by a number of fortified positions. Accordingly the brigade was to be divided: firstly a party of 300 men based around a company of the 2/5th Sherwood Foresters under Capt. Rickman was to march to Arklow south of Dublin in order to secure the arsenal and armaments factory there whilst the remainder of the battalion, along with the 2/6th, would march to Kilmainham via the Stillorgan Road. The balance of the Brigade was to take the direct – enemy-held – route to Dublin Castle.

Both columns were due to start their march at 1000hrs and, as they awaited their orders, the company officers went amongst their men, instructing them to move to the quays, face out to sea and charge, i.e. load, their weapons. Maconchy is quite adamant in his account of the brigade's actions in Ireland, that the munitions arranged by the War Office <u>had not</u> been distributed before the columns moved off, meaning that the Foresters loaded their weapons with the ready ammunition with which they had been issued before transiting to Kingstown; in other words, contrary to popular misconception, they would at least enter combat with their service rifles loaded with the correct type of ammunition for which they had been sighted.

The reason for the officers' insistence that their men load their weapons whilst facing out to sea is apparent when one considers that marksmanship was the one area in which the bulk of the troops had yet to complete their training, as Maconchy later wrote:

*It will therefore be apparent that at the time when the Brigade was called upon to fight in Ireland in this month only a very small proportion of the men had ever fired a service bullet out of their rifles … With the exception of training in musketry, the Brigade was now in a very efficient condition, thanks to the untiring energy and loyal zeal displayed by the Battalion officers and the keenness and ready response of the rank and file. Discipline was excellent and crime practically non-existent.*

# WEDNESDAY 26 APRIL – PLANS AND BLUNDERS

This third day of combat would prove to be perhaps the most crucial, not merely as a result of the fighting that took place but also because Lowe had by now formulated the tactics which the British would employ. Two cordons would be established to isolate the rebel enclaves north of the river and surround them in a 'ring of steel' whilst south of the Liffey, the bulk of the Government forces would then be directed in overwhelming force against the remaining Rebel positions.

At 0800hrs the *Helga II* and her escort, the *Sealark*, sailed back upriver and occupied berths opposite the Custom House at George's Quay and, supported by a section of 18-pdrs, began an hour-long bombardment of Liberty Hall, which was assumed to be both a concentration point for the insurgents and a major arsenal. After an hour's shelling, the guns ceased fire and the Ulster troops launched a bayonet charge from the Custom House sweeping across Beresford Place, taking a deserted Liberty Hall and sealing off one end of Lower Abbey Street and Eden Quay, which brought the troops within a few hundred yards of Sackville Street and the GPO.

**This photograph of the interior of the GPO vividly illustrates the destructive intensity of the fires that raged through central Dublin. According to a report in *The Times*, Volunteers used 'paraffin bombs' on the building before it was evacuated. (Courtesy Imperial War Museum, London – Q90444)**

Irish Rebellion, May, 1916. The General Post Office, Dublin (Rebel Headquarters) destroyed.

Across the city, similar preparations were taking place as men of the Dublin Fusiliers arranged for the evacuation of civilians preparatory to launching a major attack on the small garrison in the Mendicity Institution. Over the next three hours, the troops filed into position, harassed by rifle fire from within the building, but at 1215hrs bombing parties advanced, hurling grenades at the windows whilst other infantry followed in their wake. Initially Heuston's men were able to catch a number of grenades and hurl them back into the oncoming khaki ranks, but the British fire was too intense and casualties grew. Stunned, Heuston raised the white flag and surrendered at 1230hrs, the first of the Rebel garrisons to fall. He had been asked by Connolly to hold the position for three hours; he had held it against near insurmountable odds for almost three days.

At Trinity College, Col. Portal was again showing his industriousness. At 1400hrs machine-gun teams were sent to occupy various positions in and around D'Olier Street in order to be able to lay down suppressive fire on the Rebel positions, and then shortly afterwards he ordered his section of artillery into D'Olier Street from where he could engage an enemy strongpoint known as 'Kelly's Fort', situated on the corner of Bachelor's Walk and Sackville Street. This was an extremely hazardous proposal for the artillerymen, for not only would they be at the mercy of Volunteer snipers but also the streets were paved with large stones known as 'square setts' and all attempts to prise up the stones and expose the sand beneath to give the guns some traction failed. Thus, with their suppressors working inefficiently the gunners were expected to operate their pieces on a surface on which they would be unable to anchor the gun-trails in order to absorb some of the recoil – it was to be like deploying the guns on sheet ice.

## THE IRISH THERMOPYLAE

Moving out of Kingstown, the Sherwood Foresters were mobbed by cheering crowds who, showering the troops with gifts, demonstrated where their sympathies lay, prompting more than one enlisted man to wonder at the quality of English spoken by the inhabitants of Northern France!

One man who knew exactly where he was, however, was Captain F. C. Dietrichsen, adjutant of the 2/7th Sherwood Foresters, who, in order to escape the Zeppelin raids, had sent his wife and their children to stay with her parents in the Dublin suburb of Blackrock, and who now met them by the roadside as his men marched north, unaware of what awaited the column in the quiet suburban streets ahead.

Known as the 'Robin Hoods' the Nottinghamshire men marched towards Ballsbridge led by C Company under the command of Captain Frank Pragnell, followed by A Company under Captain H. C. Wright, and B Company under Captain H. Hanson with D Company under Captain L. L. Cooper bringing up the rear. Pragnell's command was to be deployed in a 'box' formation of platoons with one leading the advance in line abreast and one on each side of the road – in column – whose job would be to clear houses and cover all side streets, with a fourth platoon acting as support.

The battalion commander, Lieutenant-Colonel Cecil Fane, GMG DSO, attached himself to the advance party whilst the actions of the remainder of the regiment were coordinated by Major F. Rayner.

## ▼ EVENTS

1. 0800HRS, 26 APRIL **HMY *Helga II* and *Sealark II* (Q) sail upriver and anchor off George's Quay**

2. 0830HRS, 26 APRIL **Liberty Hall bombarded for one hour by *HMY Helga II* (Q) and 18-pdr guns (L) from Tara Street.**

3. 0930HRS, 26 APRIL **Composite Battalion of 15th Reserve Infantry Brigade (D) launches a bayonet attack across Beresford Place towards Eden Quay and Lower Abbey Street.**

4. 1200HRS, 26 APRIL **10th Royal Dublin Fusiliers (H) launches final attack on Rebels (3) holding the Mendicity Institution.**

5. 1215HRS, 26 APRIL **D Company, 1st (City of Dublin) Battalion, Irish Volunteers (3) surrenders after holding the Mendicity Instutution for three days.**

6. 1215HRS, 26 APRIL **2/7th (O) and 2/8th (P) Sherwood Foresters advance along Northumberland Road towards the Mount Street Bridge.**

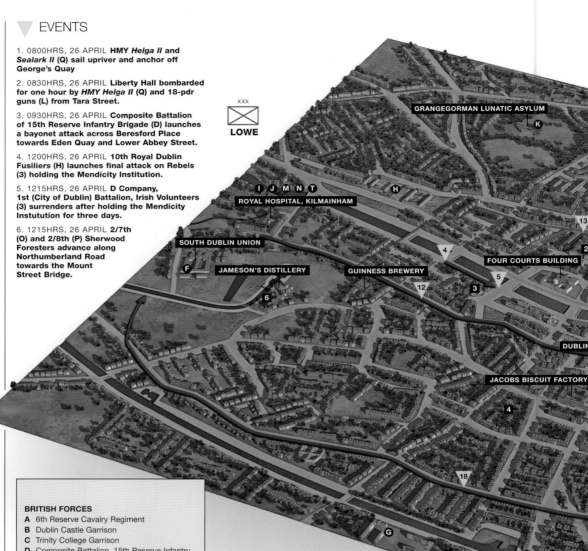

BRITISH FORCES
- A 6th Reserve Cavalry Regiment
- B Dublin Castle Garrison
- C Trinity College Garrison
- D Composite Battalion, 15th Reserve Infantry Brigade
- E Detachment, Army School of Musketry
- F 3rd Royal Irish Regiment
- G 3rd Royal Irish Rifles
- H 10th Royal Dublin Fusiliers
- I 4th Royal Dublin Fusiliers
- J Elements, 25th (Irish) Reserve Infantry Brigade
- K Section, 5th Reserve Brigade, Royal Field Artillery
- L Section, 5th Reserve Brigade, Royal Field Artillery
- M 2/5th Sherwood Foresters
- N 2/6th Sherwood Foresters
- O 2/7th Sherwood Foresters
- P 2/8th Sherwood Foresters
- Q HMY *Helga II*, Trawler *Sealark II*
- R 2/5th South Staffordshires
- S 2/6th South Staffordshires
- T 5th Leinsters
- U 8th Reserve Cavalry Regiment
- V 9th Reserve Cavalry Regiment
- W 10th Reserve Cavalry Regiment

7. 1225HRS, 26 APRIL **Sherwood Foresters ambushed in Northumberland Road, taking several casualties. The leading elements become pinned down under fire.**

8. 1240HRS, 26 APRIL **Beginning of the battle of Mount Street Bridge.**

9. 1400HRS, 26 APRIL **Troops from Trinity College (C) begin to occupy buildings in D'Olier and Westmoreland Streets and supported by artillery (L) open fire on Rebel positions opposite.**

10. 1415HRS, 26 APRIL **British cordon is completed with aggressive patrols, forcing Rebel outposts to contract in on themselves.**

11. 1900HRS, 26 APRIL **After several hours' fighting and over 300 casualties, 2/7th (O) and 2/8th (P) Sherwood Foresters clear the Insurgent positions around the Mount Street Bridge, but during the night are withdrawn from the front line, their place being taken by the 2/6th South Staffordshires (S).**

12. 0400HRS, 27 APRIL **2/5th (M) and 2/6th (N) Sherwood Foresters move from Kilmainham to Dublin Castle, and thence to the Four Courts area, coming under fire from Daly's 1st Battalion (2).**

13. 0515HRS, 27 APRIL **British begin using improvised armoured cars to transport men and materiel to reinforce the cordon around the Volunteers Headquarters (1) and 1st Battalion (2) positions.**

14. 0900HRS, 27 APRIL **2/5th (R) and 2/6th (S) Sherwood Foresters begin street-clearing operations in the north of the western cordon.**

15. 1000HRS, 27 APRIL **Firing random shots, British artillery begins to shell Sackville Street area. 18-pdr shell hits the Irish *Times*' paper store, igniting several rolls of newsprint.**

16. 1030HRS, 27 APRIL **As the fire begins to spread, British troops move forward under the cover of smoke but are stopped by fire from Middle Abbey Street.**

17. 1200HRS, 27 APRIL **2/5th (R) and 2/6th (S) South Staffordshires push forward along Lower Mount Street towards Trinity College, establishing sniper positions that engage de Valera's 3rd Battalion (5) until the early evening.**

# CONSOLIDATION

The containment of the Rebel positions, Wednesday 26-Thursday 27 April 1916.

This map is 4.4 x 3km

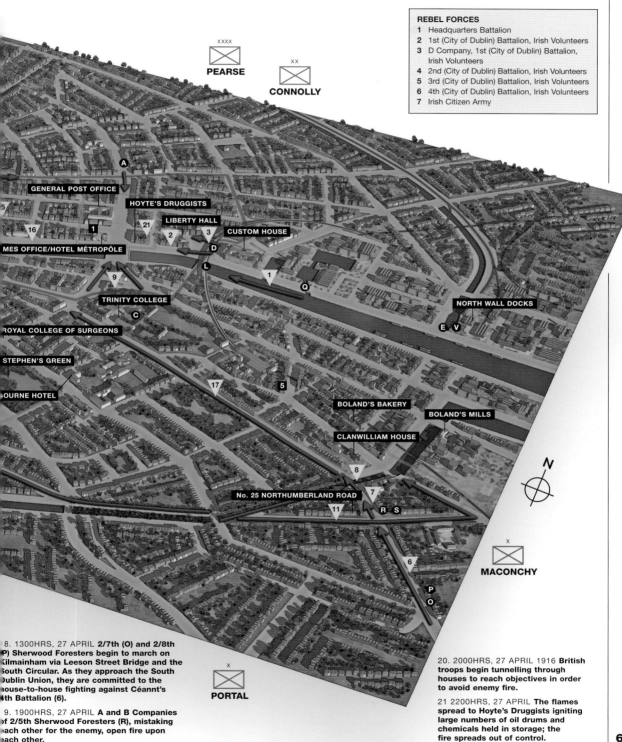

**REBEL FORCES**
1 Headquarters Battalion
2 1st (City of Dublin) Battalion, Irish Volunteers
3 D Company, 1st (City of Dublin) Battalion, Irish Volunteers
4 2nd (City of Dublin) Battalion, Irish Volunteers
5 3rd (City of Dublin) Battalion, Irish Volunteers
6 4th (City of Dublin) Battalion, Irish Volunteers
7 Irish Citizen Army

xxxx
**PEARSE**

xx
**CONNOLLY**

GENERAL POST OFFICE

HOYTE'S DRUGGISTS

LIBERTY HALL

CUSTOM HOUSE

MES OFFICE/HOTEL MÉTROPÔLE

TRINITY COLLEGE

ROYAL COLLEGE OF SURGEONS

STEPHEN'S GREEN

OURNE HOTEL

NORTH WALL DOCKS

BOLAND'S BAKERY

BOLAND'S MILLS

CLANWILLIAM HOUSE

No. 25 NORTHUMBERLAND ROAD

x
**MACONCHY**

x
**PORTAL**

8. 1300HRS, 27 APRIL **2/7th (O) and 2/8th (P) Sherwood Foresters begin to march on Kilmainham via Leeson Street Bridge and the South Circular. As they approach the South Dublin Union, they are committed to the house-to-house fighting against Céannt's 4th Battalion (6).**

9. 1900HRS, 27 APRIL **A and B Companies of 2/5th Sherwood Foresters (R), mistaking each other for the enemy, open fire upon each other.**

20. 2000HRS, 27 APRIL 1916 **British troops begin tunnelling through houses to reach objectives in order to avoid enemy fire.**

21 2200HRS, 27 APRIL **The flames spread to Hoyte's Druggists igniting large numbers of oil drums and chemicals held in storage; the fire spreads out of control.**

After an interval of 400 yards came the 2/8th Sherwood Foresters under the command of Lieutenant-Colonel W. C. Oates marching in a similar formation though without a rearguard company as a result of the involuntary detachment of D Company under Captain J. Oates, the battalion commander's son.

By midday the column had reached Ballsbridge, where a joint headquarters was established for both the 177th and 178th Brigades in the nearby Pembroke Town Hall. The troops were given 15 minutes' rest whilst Maconchy conferred with his two battalion commanders. The latest information from Irish Command was that heavy opposition was to be expected in the area around the Mount Street Canal Bridge, and that the rebels had fortified a schoolhouse on the right-hand side of the road.

Shortly after the troops resumed their march a number of shots rang out from nearby Carisbrooke House, forcing them to take evasive action, but under their company officers, the men reacted calmly and efficiently. The ambushers soon melted away however, and Lt. Col. Fane gave the order for the advance to continue, albeit more cautiously, and he led D Company into Northumberland Road whilst Maj. Rayner and the bulk of the battalion followed at a reasonable distance.

Ahead, and covering the approaches to the Mount Street Canal Bridge, a detachment of de Valera's 3rd Volunteer Battalion had occupied a number of houses in Northumberland Road in order to cover the direct route towards Dublin Castle and Trinity College.

The projected killing zone was rectangular in shape and stretched from the canal bridge to the junction of Northumberland Road with Haddington Road and Cranmer Street, and comprised four separate firing positions. As the troops proceeded towards the bridge, they would be met by fire from No. 25, on their left flank, which was occupied by Lieutenant Michael Malone – a crack shot, and one of de Valera's best officers – and James Grace, again an expert marksman who had deserted from a Territorial unit in Canada to take part in the Rising. Two additional Volunteers had originally made up the garrison but, aware that there would be little chance of his party's survival, Malone sent them back to battalion HQ.

Farther along the left-hand side of the road at No. 5, which was occupied by five men, was a red brick building used as a Hall for the Parochial School which was opposite at No. 10. The school itself had been initially occupied by a small party but was evacuated and the occupants divided between the Parochial Hall and the final position, Clanwilliam House, a building standing on the far side of the bridge at the corner of Lower Mount Street and the Grand Canal Quay. In each of the positions, the doors and lower floor windows were barricaded in order to deny the enemy access, whilst the Volunteers were to fire from the upper floors using the added elevation to engage the length of the British column, thereby increasing the confusion.

All told, a dozen or so men lay in wait for the approaching troops. The plan was simple, to let the leading British elements pass unmolested and then when Malone and Grace opened fire it would act as a signal for the remaining positions to engage the enemy, trapping them in a crossfire that would hopefully disorient them and belie the Volunteers' lack of numbers.

Inexorably the khaki-clad soldiers advanced, their formation constricted by the width of the road, nervously scanning the lines of

suburban houses for signs of anything untoward, first one company and then another moving into the killing zone.

Upstairs in No. 25, Malone and Grace watched the troops pass below their position. Silently nodding to his partner, Malone aimed his Mauser C96 semi-automatic pistol out of the window and emptied the 10-shot magazine into the street below. As he ducked back inside, Grace fired several shots in quick succession at another section of the column and after a momentary delay the other positions began to open fire at the British infantrymen who had instinctively dropped to the ground. Among the first to fall was Capt. Dietrichsen, who tragically had been reunited with his family scant hours before.

Waiting until there was a slackening in the enemy fire, Fane and Pragnell got to their feet and, with drawn swords, led the men immediately around them in a charge on the entrance to No. 25.

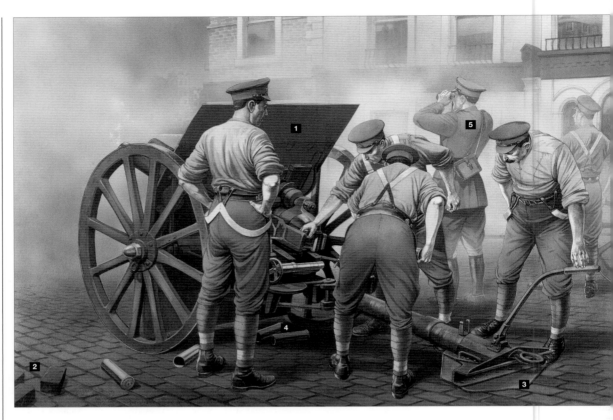

## THE BOMBARDMENT OF LIBERTY HALL, 25 APRIL 1916.
(Pages 66-67)

In the mistaken belief that the Rebel headquarters was situated at Liberty Hall in Beresford Place, adjacent to the Custom House, the British Commander, Brig. Lowe, ordered the building to be bombarded. At 0800hrs the yacht *Helga II* anchored on the southern bank of the river Liffey, and made preparations to shell the Beresford Place area whilst, at the same time the section of two 18-pdr field guns (1) were ordered from Trinity College to Tara Street from where they could fire upon Liberty Hall under open sights. A small side road leading down to the Liffey, Tara Street was a far from ideal position from which to conduct an artillery bombardment. Narrow, and closely paved with stones known as 'square setts', it proved almost impossible for the British gunners to properly deploy their weapons and several fruitless attempts were then made to dig up the paving blocks (2) in order to expose the sand underneath and thereby give the gunners a means by which they could fix their pieces in position. Accordingly, the gunners were unable to anchor their guns (3) and as a result their severe recoil went unchecked, necessitating

that the pieces be re-sited after each shell was fired. The only rounds available to the field guns were fixed shrapnel (4), an anti-personnel shell that had negligible effect against most buildings. As the bombardment continued, the narrow street began to fill with smoke generated by the gunfire, and the resulting lack of visibility added to the problems already being experienced by the artillerymen. The unit commander (5) is shown here attempting to observe the fall of shot and assess the damage being done to the target. Given the angle of fire from both British positions, it is generally assumed that the high-explosive shells fired from *Helga II* were directed against a building adjacent to Liberty Hall, which was largely destroyed during the bombardment, whilst the fire from the field artillery was aimed at Liberty Hall, which itself suffered minor exterior damage (see the photograph on page 73). After an hour the bombardment was called off with the British commanders being mistakenly convinced that the Rebel headquarters had been destroyed, and it may be conjectured that this belief was in fact a contributing factor in Lowe's plan to isolate and 'quarantine' the various Rebel positions.

Ruins of Eden Quay. The buildings at the corner of Sackville Street and Eden Quay had been shelled by British artillery firing from D'Olier Street, and were then overwhelmed by the conflagration that originated in the Hoyte's Drug Company building. (Courtesy Imperial War Museum, London – Q90446)

As they reached the stairwell, the two Irishmen had completed their reloading and poured a deadly volley into the milling troops. Taking this as their cue, the other company officers had formed their men for an assault on the bridge, but this was broken up when the column was hit by fire from Clanwilliam House and almost immediately enfiladed by the men holding the Parochial Hall.

With the attack stalled, Fane detached Capt. Hanson's B Company south-west toward the Baggot Street Bridge, with orders to outflank the ambushers by doubling back along the canal bank; as the young soldiers moved off, Malone moved into the bathroom and twice emptied his Mauser into the group of men, wreaking havoc in their tightly packed ranks. Luckily, Hanson's men were soon out of Malone's line of fire and cautiously made their way to the bridge convinced that a second ambush would be sprung at any moment. Leaving a platoon to guard the crossing, the remainder of the company began to move eastwards along Percy Place.

At the crossroads the situation was becoming desperate; fire was being directed at the four corner houses although only one – No. 25 – was occupied by the enemy. Then, disaster struck as Fane was hit in the left arm and severely wounded. Waving away assistance he calmly handed over command to Maj. Rayner and only then consented to withdraw to cover and accept treatment; standing in the middle of the road giving orders, the new commander seemed to lead a charmed life, his uniform being literally shredded by rifle fire.

The fighting had been going on for a little over an hour, but despite the heavy casualties and their unpreparednesss, the Foresters were grimly holding on. A number of houses opposite Malone and Grace's position were now occupied and a steady, if ineffectual, fire began to be poured in their direction, the volume lending encouragement to the raw troops.

Irish Rebellion, May, 1916.
The wreck they made of Church Street, Dublin.

Along the canal bank in Percy Place, Hanson's men were soon spotted and a galling fire opened up from the side windows of Clanwilliam House. The soldiers went to ground almost immediately, but the coping stones lining the towpath gave them inadequate cover, and their opponents were literally able to track the khaki uniforms as they inched forwards towards the Mount Street Bridge. The company commander and his two subordinate officers were early casualties but the men continued to advance under the orders of a senior NCO; however, as they reached the bridge they came under the sights of another of de Valera's defensive positions and the flanking manoeuvre was stopped dead in its tracks.

Fane then decided to try to turn the enemy position from the east, and directed Capt. Wright to move his men around via Beggars Bush Barracks. Almost immediately the manoeuvre came into difficulty as the barracks commander, Colonel Sir Frederick Shaw, commandeered one of the platoons to assist in defending his compound. This attempt to turn the Volunteers' position also came to naught as Wright's men came under fire from an enemy outpost in Boland's Mills on Grand Canal Quay. In retrospect the men were fortunate as, if they had managed to cross the canal at this point, they would have blundered into the sights of de Valera's main position at Boland's Bakery in Grand Canal Street.

At 1445hrs Lt. Col. Fane reported to Brigade HQ that, although his men were pinned down by enemy fire and that all attempts so far to turn the position had been thwarted, if given machine-gun support and a number of grenades he still might be able to push through to the objective. Following a suggestion from Irish Command, the Bombing School at Elm Park was contacted and the commander, Captain Jeffares, volunteered himself and a number of his men to assist the column, giving Maconchy some much-needed expertise in the use of grenades and explosives.

Wreckage in Church Street. British troops attempt to clear the wreckage of a rebel barricade from the debris surrounding the junction of Church Street and Arran Quay. (Courtesy Imperial War Museum, London – Q90447)

The Sherwood Foresters were rapidly running out of options, and Fane decided to make another attempt. Capt. Cooper's D Company, which had lain in reserve until now, was brought forwards and the men deployed around the crossroads, whilst the survivors of Pragnell's men were withdrawn and ordered to move via Percy Lane – an alley parallel to Northumberland Road – and reinforce Hanson's company. Again, Malone was waiting for the troops to move and, before they passed from view, accounted for another dozen or so soldiers. In Northumberland Road meanwhile, the front of the house was the target for a whole company of British troops, mistakenly aiming for the unoccupied ground and first-floor windows, even as their officers' whistles summoned their men for another assault on the bridge.

For Maconchy it was now clear that his remaining battalion would need to be committed if the situation were to be salvaged. Accordingly, Lt. Col. Oates of the 2/8th was ordered to advance along the road with two of his three companies present and to detach A Company under Captain Quinnell in another attempt to turn the Volunteers' left flank. Even as the troops were forming up another message was received from Brig. Lowe at Kilmainham, rescinding permission for the flanking manoeuvre – the bridge was to be taken at the point of the bayonet!

At the head of Percy Lane, Pragnell readied his company for a sprint towards the objective, but as they left cover they ran straight into the sights of the men who had earlier so effectively halted B Company's advance; badly wounded, Pragnell almost made it, followed by a mere six men but the fire was too great. Fane's battalion was shattered, with two companies pinned down in Percy Place and a third being flayed by enemy volleys as it attempted to force its way across the narrow bridge; it was all that he could do to hold on until reinforcements arrived.

A short distance away at Boland's Bakery, the men of de Valera's 3rd Battalion could only listen to the sounds of gunfire as their comrades fought against the advancing troops. Despite the failure of the flanking manoeuvres, the fact that the attempts had been made had persuaded de Valera that he couldn't afford to send any men to reinforce those engaged at the Mount Street Bridge. This was a missed opportunity, as even a token gesture could have had disastrous consequences for Fane's men.

By 1700hrs the fighting began to move inexorably to its climax. With the arrival of Capt. Jeffares preparations were being made for an assault on No. 25 – grenades were thrown through broken windows and then, under the cover of the explosions and sustained rifle fire from the houses opposite, the front door was blown in. With the entrance in ruins, there was inexplicably no attempt to immediately carry the building and Grace and Malone kept up their harassment of the troops below until finally a section of D Company charged across the street. As soon as they had seen the troops forming up, Grace had gone downstairs and waited for Malone to join him, but the soldiers swarming into the house prevented their junction. Diving for the cellar, Grace snapped off a few quick shots at the milling infantrymen but an answering volley felled Malone as he stood at the top of the stairs. The British then threw a number of grenades into the cellar to take care of Grace, but he took cover behind an old gas cooker, and remained hidden until the fighting had moved on and he was able to escape in the darkness.

With No. 25 neutralized, Oates held a hurried officers' call. B Company would spearhead the attack, closely supported by A Company with C Company acting as a general reserve to exploit any potential success. Rushing up Northumberland Road, the 2/8th were soon taking casualties. Without orders and following their sister battalion came a platoon of D Company, 2/7th, under the command of Lieutenant Foster. These unlooked-for reinforcements forced their way into the Old Schoolhouse at the top of the road, and took up positions from which they could engage Clanwilliam House. Foster was exasperated by his men's fire, crying, 'How is it that normally the platoon has plenty of excellent marksmen and first-class shots and yet now you can't hit a whole terrace at 50 yards' range?'

Breaking cover, B Company stormed across the bridge but was halted just short of the target with both of its officers being killed shortly after reaching the northern bank.

For the defenders however, the importance of Malone and Grace to the ambush now became apparent as, without their support and in the face of increasing numbers of British troops, the men in the Parochial Hall evacuated their position and were captured in Percy Lane. It was a minor success that would make Maconchy's task only marginally easier.

With the southern side of the bridge cleared, Oates began to deploy troops in buildings and behind walls to give the men a direct line of fire on Clanwilliam House massing the rest of his troops in the lee of a stone advertising hoarding at the top of Northumberland Road. The plan, such as it was, was that the column would storm across the bridge and overrun the Rebel position. Indeed it was much the same as all other – failed – attempts to secure the crossing but this time the troops would be preceded by a number of their comrades throwing bombs into Clanwilliam House and supported by the platoons who were now in possession of several buildings from which they would be able to lay down a heavy, suppressive volume of fire into the enemy strongpoint. Accuracy was not the issue, it was merely sufficient to keep the enemy's heads down so that the column could close and storm the building.

Detail of 'square setts', Trinity College. The paving around Trinity College proved to be almost impervious to all attempts to prise up the stones and give the British field artillery some form of purchase to absorb the recoil of their guns. (Courtesy David Murphy)

This photograph shows Liberty Hall after an hour-long bombardment by British forces. Explosive shells from HMY *Helga II* have presumably hit the building to the right, whilst Liberty Hall itself has been targeted by field artillery from Tara Street. A comparison of the damage suffered by both buildings gives testament to the usefulness of the 18-pdr shells against fixed positions. (Courtesy National Museum of Ireland, Dublin)

In the end it was an unnecessary precaution as the bombs ignited the house's gas supply and the building was soon wreathed in flames with the majority of its occupants being able to make their escape in the confusion. With the area backlit by flame, the Sherwood Foresters began to consolidate their hard-won position and prepare to make the final push on Dublin Castle at daybreak, but as night progressed a message was received ordering the men back to Ballsbridge and their positions were taken over by Brig. Carleton's 177th Brigade, which consisted of the four Staffordshire battalions.

## THURSDAY 27 APRIL – A CITY IN FLAMES

As dawn broke, the city fell back into what had become its normal state – British troops slowly pushing forwards only to be met by rifle fire from the Rebel positions, whilst from vantage points and rooftops snipers engaged each other in a deadly game of cat and mouse.

At 1000hrs, the calm was shattered as field guns began to fire shells into the Sackville Street area. Although the guns were undoubtedly firing at maximum elevation and without spotters, they were soon to have a crucial influence on the battle; shortly after they opened fire a number of shells plunged into a warehouse owned by the *Irish Times*. Despite the fact that the munitions used by the 18-pdrs were intended as anti-personnel weapons, the building was filled with combustible materials and all it took was a single spark to ignite them. As the flames took hold they began to spread in all directions, not just to neighbouring buildings but also across some of the hastily erected Rebel barricades, themselves constructed of furniture and paper bales taken from the warehouse. From the roof of the

## THE BATTLE OF MOUNT STREET CANAL BRIDGE, 25 APRIL 1916. (Pages 74-75)

Having been ordered to march by the most direct route to the Dublin Castle area, the Sherwood Foresters entered Northumberland Road cautiously, but fully aware that somewhere along their route lay a Rebel ambush. At first, all seemed to go well but then, as the rearmost elements of the 2/7th Battalion passed No. 25 – on the corner with Haddington Road – the jaws of the trap snapped shut. Positioned at upper storey windows (1), Lt. Michael Malone and Section-Leader James Grace opened fire on the soldiers packing the roadway below them, mortally wounding the battalion adjutant, Capt. F. C. Dietrichsen (2). This was the signal for Volunteers in other buildings to start firing at the stationary troops. In the resulting confusion, and fired upon from several directions at once, the British troops returned fire on a number of houses closest to them, most of which were unoccupied (3). Having survived the initial shock, Lt. Col. Fane (4) and Capt. Pragnell (5) rallied their men, and led a charge against Malone and Grace's position in No. 25 (6), unaware that the doors and lower windows had been heavily barricaded to prevent the troops from storming the house, and as they crossed the road the were caught in an enfilade fire (7) by other ambush positions further up Northumberland Road. The British advance had by now ground to a complete halt, with the troops focussed on securing the Mount Street Canal Bridge – a fixation that led to alternate crossing points such as the Baggot Street Bridge being ignored. For several hours, a small number of Volunteers inflicted horrendous casualties on the Foresters until, at almost 2000hrs, they were able to bludgeon their way across the Mount Street Canal Bridge, carrying the final ambush position at Clanwilliam House, and opening the route into the city, having suffered – in this single engagement – almost half of the total casualties received by the British forces during the whole of the Easter Rising. The experience of the Foresters in Northumberland Road undoubtedly gave rise to a more cautious approach being exhibited by British forces during the latter half of the Rising, causing local commanders to adopt a more systematic approach during the street-clearing operations which took place as the cordon was completed.

The side entrance to Trinity College from which the field artillery were deployed, first into Tara Street to bombard Liberty Hall, and subsequently to D'Olier Street to engage Rebel positions at the southern end of Sackville Street. (Courtesy David Murphy)

GPO, sentries reported a number of fires as having been started by British incendiary shells but, given the British ammunition limitations, a more reasonable explanation is that these fires were caused by burning debris falling from the Métropole Hotel on the opposite side of Princes Street.

At the GPO, James Connolly was seemingly everywhere at once – issuing orders and responding to reports from the various outposts and it was whilst overseeing the construction of a barricade in Princes Street that he was hit by British fire. Draping his jacket over the wound he then went up to Captain Mahony, a British prisoner who was assisting the medical staff, and, ducking behind a screen, asked him to dress the wound. Later on during the afternoon, he was overseeing the occupation of a new position in Middle Abbey Street when disaster struck – a bullet

Led by the tall figure of Eamon de Valera, the men of the 3rd (Dublin City) Battalion march into captivity. As they came into Grand Canal Street they were met by a standing ovation from assembled onlookers, before surrendering their arms to the British in Grattan Street. (Courtesy National Museum of Ireland, Dublin – HE4702/B205)

The surrender of P. H. Pearse (right) to Brig. W. H. M. Lowe. This meeting, which took place at 1430hrs on 29 April, merely confirmed Pearse's desire to discuss surrender terms. The actual instrument of surrender was signed by Pearse and Maxwell later that afternoon, and was additionally endorsed by James Connolly. (Courtesy National Museum of Ireland, Dublin – HE1185/B273)

ricocheted off the pavement and smashed into his ankle. In agony, he crawled back into Princes Street where he was found and carried into the GPO. This time there was no possibility of concealing either the wound or its severity, and he was propped up on a mattress in the public hall.

From Kilmainham the 2/5th and 2/6th Sherwood Foresters were ordered to Capel Street to reinforce the cordon and commence street-clearing operations. Supporting the troops were two improvised personnel carriers, which had been built at the Inchicore Iron Works during the previous afternoon. Two flatbed lorries had been fitted with boilers supplied by the Guinness Brewery and, drilled with loopholes and vision slits, they provided adequate protection for the transport of troops and supplies. As they reached their destination, they began an almost textbook street-clearing exercise with each company being allocated to a fixed area and each platoon or section within the company being likewise assigned to specific streets and houses. Once the men were established and operations begun, the armoured cars were used to bring back the artillery from the Grangegorman Asylum, which was then used in a direct support role against known enemy positions.

A few streets away from Clanwilliam House, the majority of de Valera's 3rd Volunteer Battalion had spent an uneasy night with several false alarms of British attacks, a number of which were simply the product of their commander's imagination. At midday the 2/5th and 2/6th South Staffordshires recommenced the drive towards Trinity College and, tempered by the events of the preceding afternoon, they were content to isolate the Volunteers by dropping off sniper teams en route whose task was to engage de Valera's men and hold them in position until additional troops followed up. The irony of the situation is that had the Staffordshires made a more resolute showing they would have most likely swamped the rebel positions and destroyed the 3rd Battalion as a fighting force. The truth of the matter is that they were both untrained in street fighting and unaware of the meagre size of the opposing forces.

Still recovering from their ordeal of the previous day, and by now reunited with the errant D Company, 2/8th Battalion, the remainder of the 178th Brigade received orders to move around the south of the city to Kilmainham and, as news had been received that the remainder of the brigade had reached that same destination without incident, a fresh optimism had begun to permeate the ranks.

INTERIOR OF THE GPO BUILDING, c.1430HRS, 27 APRIL 1916

As neighbouring buildings in Princes Street begin to smoulder, we see here the situation within the eastern or A Block of the General Post Office. Following the excitement of the attack on the British cavalry on Easter Monday, the garrison has now reverted into a more reactive mode in anticipation of a British assault on the building. Despite being wounded earlier on in the day, here we see James Connolly (1) giving orders to Lt. Oscar Traynor for the establishment of a new outpost in Middle Abbey Street. It was whilst overseeing this operation that a ricocheting bullet shattered Connolly's ankle. Sheltered behind the main counter, a Volunteer mans an ad-hoc arsenal (2), whilst a captured British officer Capt. George Mahoney, attends to the wounded in a makeshift hospital area (3). To protect the main entrance to the public hall, the main doors are being barricaded (4) whilst a number of Volunteers and ICA men man the windows (5). Upstairs, Tom Clarke and Seán MacDermott have taken over one of the offices (6), where a signaller uses a tin can tied to a length of twine (7) to carry messages between the GPO and the Rebel positions on the opposite side of Sackville Street. From the balustrade several sentries (8) watch anxiously for signs of movement by the British forces, whilst two men guard the entrance to the van yard (9). Following Connolly's wounding the scene would change dramatically as flaming debris set light to the upper storeys of the building eventually blazing out of control and ultimately forcing the Headquarters Battalion to abandon its positions during the Friday evening.

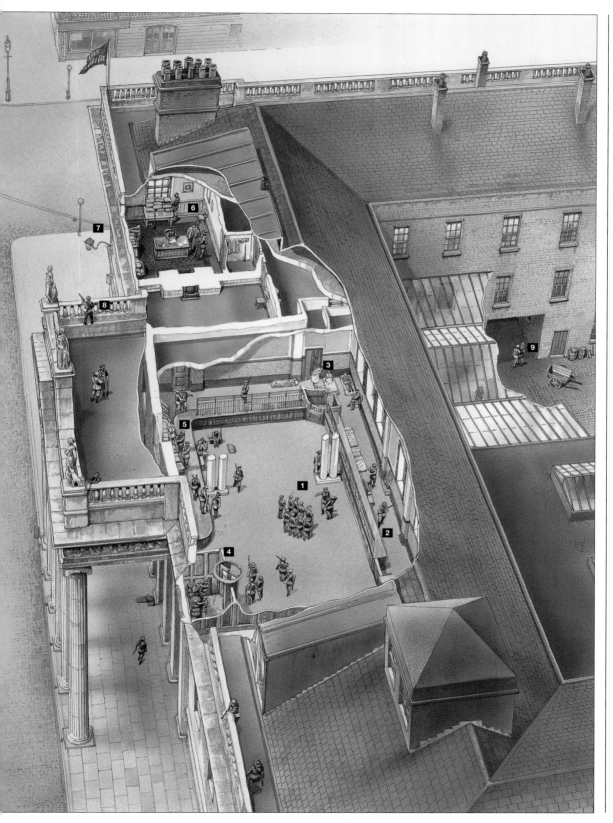

At 1300hrs, and with Lt. Col. Oates' battalion in the lead, the column broke camp and began the march westwards through the southern suburbs. As anticipated, their progress was uneventful, but, as the leading elements made to cross the Rialto Bridge that would take them into the southern part of the South Dublin Union, Céannt's outposts fired upon them and the troops went to ground. The situation was an ominous echo of the previous afternoon's attack in Northumberland Road, but here the terrain was more open and the British forces were able to clear a way through to the South Dublin Union.

Oates then sent his second in command, Captain 'Mickey' Martyn to move into the buildings at the head of an aggressive patrol to engage the enemy whilst the rest of the column pushed ahead to Kilmainham. The men came under enemy fire almost as soon as they entered the grounds, with Martyn noting that:

> *I found that a bullet in Dublin was every bit as dangerous as one in No-Man's Land … In some ways the fighting in Dublin was worse – In France you had a fair idea of where the enemy was and where the bullets were going to come from. In Dublin you never knew when or from where you were going to be hit.*

The British troops slowly made their way into the complex, but the volume and accuracy of the Volunteers' fire was a testament of how well Céannt had deployed his few men. Gathering any tools they could find, the Foresters tunnelled their way from room to room. As they broke into the Nurses Home, Martyn went forwards with a Sergeant Walker to clear the way ahead with bombs, being joined by Capt. Oates as they successfully turned one of the enemy barricades that had been built in several of the buildings.

On the other side of the firing line, things were becoming critical. Of his initial force Céannt had lost over 20 men killed and wounded with a further dozen having been captured as the British infantry applied their inexorable pressure against his defences. And now the long-range sniping that had characterized the early stages of the fighting in the Union had given way to a series of close-quarter engagements. Céannt realized that he had no effective response to the enemy's superior numbers and firepower and decided that the best course of action would be to fight in the enclosed rooms and corridors in the hope that the confusion would cause the British to miscalculate the defenders' strength. The situation had almost became moot however, when Céannt narrowly escaped being shot as the British broke into the Nurses Home, soon afterwards his deputy, Cathal Brugha, was hit several times and critically wounded.

The morale of the men of the 4th Battalion had now reached an all-time low. The euphoria of the first day's fighting had given way to the relentless pressure of the succeeding days, and now it seemed as if all were lost with many believing that they should wait for the British to take them prisoner. What saved the situation was the badly wounded Brugha, who had put himself into a position from which he could interdict the British advance and was now singing Republican songs at the top of his voice. The singing lifted the men from their lethargy and they rushed back to man the barricade. On the other side of the doorway waited

Soldiers guarding the entrance to Trinity College following the suppression of the Rising. The man on the right of the picture is obviously on guard duty whilst his colleagues are merely posing for the camera. (Courtesy Imperial War Museum, London – HU55528)

Oates and one of his platoons, both groups nervously holding their position in the belief that an enemy attack was imminent. For over an hour the situation rested on a knife-edge but then, as darkness fell, a message came from battalion HQ that the column had broken through to the Royal Hospital and that Oates was to withdraw. For the second time that day the British forces had come within an ace of eliminating one of the Volunteer battalions only to pull back at the moment of truth.

As night fell, a red haze lay over the centre of Dublin. The fire begun in the *Irish Times'* warehouse had now spread into several neighbouring areas and the glow was echoed by that above the Linenhall Barracks, which had earlier been set alight by men of Daly's 1st Battalion. At 2200hrs this all, literally, paled into insignificance when Hoyte's Druggists and Oil Works, which lay on the opposite side of Sackville Street, exploded in a column of flame scattering flaming debris over a wide area.

The situation within the GPO was becoming critical, small fires had started on the roof and now the surrounding buildings were awash with flame as fire hoses were deployed to douse any surfaces that looked as if they might catch fire. In the public hall, Connolly was propped up on a mattress still masterminding the Volunteers' defence, supported by the rest of the Provisional Government who had by now all congregated in this central area.

## FRIDAY 28 APRIL – THE BEGINNING OF THE END

At 0200hrs on Friday morning, a small group of men disembarked from a British warship that had tied up against the North Wall Quay; ushered

## ▼ EVENTS

1. 0001HRS, 28 APRIL **The blaze that originated in the *Times* Building and Hoyte's Druggists is now beginning to spread out of control as the Dublin Fire Brigade has been effectively stood down due to the danger from indiscriminate small-arms fire.**

2. 0200HRS, 28 APRIL **General Sir John Maxwell arrives at North Wall Docks to assume command of the British forces.**

3. 1000HRS, 28 APRIL **The newly arrived 2/4th Lincolns ordered to assist in throwing a cordon around de Valera's 3rd Battalion (6), taking over from the 2/6th South Staffordshires (S).**

4. 1000HRS, 28 APRIL **Maxwell orders the 2/5th (R) and 2/6th (S) South Staffordshires to move from Trinity College in on the Four Courts area.**

5. 1020HRS, 28 APRIL **2/5th (M) and 2/6th (N) Sherwood Foresters and the 3rd Royal Irish Regiment (F) are ordered to close in on the GPO from the west and the 5th Leinsters join the eastern cordon.**

**MAXWELL** xxxx

**LOWE** xxx

**MACONCHY** x

**PORTAL** x

GRANGEGORMAN LUNATIC ASYLUM

ROYAL HOSPITAL, KILMAINHAM  F I J O P Z

SOUTH DUBLIN UNION

JAMESON'S DISTILLERY

GUINNESS BREWERY

FOUR COURTS BUILDING  2

A

H

CITY

DUBLIN CASTL

JACOBS BISCUIT FACTORY

3

5

G

### BRITISH FORCES

| | |
|---|---|
| A | 6th Reserve Cavalry Regiment |
| B | Dublin Castle Garrison |
| C | Trinity College Garrison |
| D | Composite Battalion, 15th Reserve Infantry Brigade |
| E | Detachment, Army School of Musketry |
| F | 3rd Royal Irish Regiment |
| G | 3rd Royal Irish Rifles |
| H | 10th Royal Dublin Fusiliers |
| I | 4th Royal Dublin Fusiliers |
| J | Elements, 25th (Irish) Reserve Infantry Brigade |
| K | Section, 5th Reserve Brigade, Royal Field Artillery |
| L | Section, 5th Reserve Brigade, Royal Field Artillery |
| M | 2/5th Sherwood Foresters |
| N | 2/6th Sherwood Foresters |
| O | 2/7th Sherwood Foresters |
| P | 2/8th Sherwood Foresters |
| Q | HMY *Helga II*/Trawler *Sealark II* |
| R | 2/5th South Staffordshires |
| S | 2/6th South Staffordshires |
| T | 2/5th North Staffordshires |
| U | 2/6th North Staffordshires |
| V | 2/4th Leicesters |
| W | 2/5th Leicesters |
| X | 2/4th Lincolns |
| Y | 2/5th Lincolns |
| Z | 5th Leinsters |
| AA | 8th Reserve Cavalry Regiment |
| AB | 9th Reserve Cavalry Regiment |
| AC | 10th Reserve Cavalry Regiment |

6. 1030HRS, 28 APRIL **3rd Royal Irish Regiment (F) occupies Great Britain Street.**

7. 1155HRS, 28 APRIL **An 18-pdr field gun (K) is brought up to the corner of Great Britain Street and Coles Lane. The shellfire starts a small blaze in Arnott's store in Henry Street, which is extinguished by the building's sprinkler system.**

8. 1900HRS, 28 APRIL **The Headquarters Battalion (1) is unable to extinguish the fire that has taken hold of the GPO. The Provisional Government agrees to evacuate the building in favour of a new headquarters at Williams & Woods in Great Britain Street.**

9. 2000HRS, 28 APRIL **The O'Rahilly leads a sortie from the GPO to clear a British barricade in Moore Street but his men are cut to pieces, and he himself is mortally wounded.**

10. 2000HRS, 28 APRIL **The Headquarters Battalion (1) pulls in its outlying positions preparatory to staging a breakout to the new Headquarters at Williams & Woods.**

11. 2015HRS, 28 APRIL **The Headquarters Battalion (1) is forced to take shelter in No. 15 Moore Street and attempts to tunnel through to Great Britain Street.**

12. 1100HRS, 29 APRIL **The 3rd Royal Irish Regiment (F) reinforced by 100 men of 2/6th Sherwood Foresters (N) prepares to assault the ruins of the GPO.**

13. 1245HRS, 29 APRIL **To avoid further civilian casualties, the Provisional Government aggress to establish contact with the British commander to discuss surrender terms.**

14. 1430HRS, 29 APRIL **Brigadier Lowe meets Pearse at the British barricade in Moore Street. The terms given are unconditional surrender. Countersigned by James Connolly, the order is to be brought to the battalion commanders by Nurse Elizabeth O'Farrell and Lowe's ADC, Captain de Courcey-Wheeler. Although it will take several hours before all insurgent forces comply with the surrender orders, the Rising is effectively at an end.**

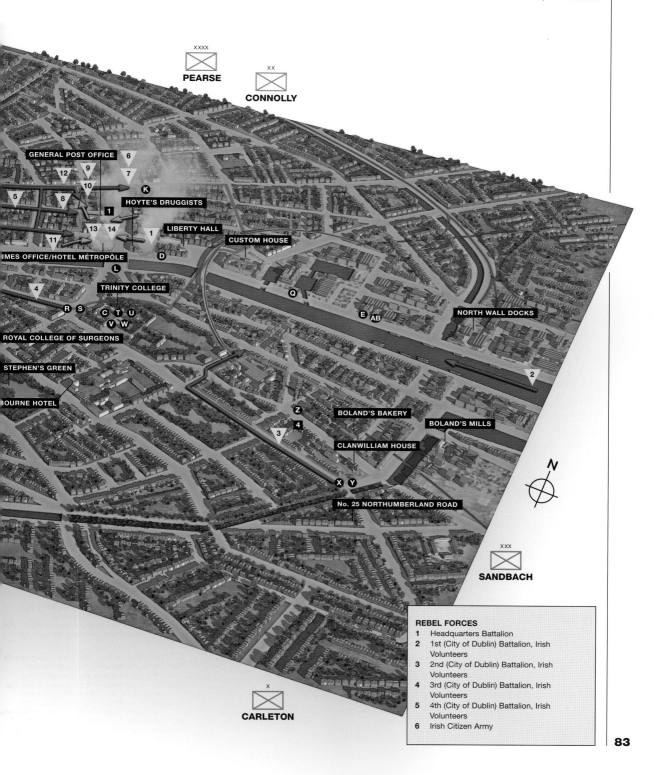

# THE FINAL CURTAIN

The British cordon and the failed breakout attempt, Friday 28-Saturday 29 April 1916.

This map is 4.4 x 3km

**PEARSE** xxxx

**CONNOLLY** xx

**GENERAL POST OFFICE**    6
12    9
      10    7
5    8    K
      1    **HOYTE'S DRUGGISTS**
13    14    **LIBERTY HALL**
11    1    **CUSTOM HOUSE**
IMES OFFICE/HOTEL MÉTROPÔLE    D
L

4    **TRINITY COLLEGE**    Q
R    S    C    T    U    E    AB    **NORTH WALL DOCKS**
      V    W
**ROYAL COLLEGE OF SURGEONS**

**STEPHEN'S GREEN**
                                                    2
BOURNE HOTEL

Z    **BOLAND'S BAKERY**
4    **BOLAND'S MILLS**
3    **CLANWILLIAM HOUSE**

X    Y
**No. 25 NORTHUMBERLAND ROAD**

N

**SANDBACH** xxx

**CARLETON** x

**REBEL FORCES**
1    Headquarters Battalion
2    1st (City of Dublin) Battalion, Irish Volunteers
3    2nd (City of Dublin) Battalion, Irish Volunteers
4    3rd (City of Dublin) Battalion, Irish Volunteers
5    4th (City of Dublin) Battalion, Irish Volunteers
6    Irish Citizen Army

into three waiting motor cars they were driven to Kilmainham Hospital – General Sir John Maxwell KCB KCMG had arrived to assume his position as general officer commanding, Ireland.

Maxwell quickly reaffirmed Lowe's existing dispositions and orders, and gave additional instructions for the 2/5th and 2/6th South Staffordshires to move across the Liffey to reduce the Four Courts area whilst the remainder of Carleton's 177th Brigade and the leading elements of the 176th (Lincoln and Leicester) Brigade were to deploy to contain the area occupied by de Valera's troops.

Unlike the previous two days, dawn seemed to be a bit of an anti-climax with no great demonstrations, but those with field glasses or telescopes could see small knots of khaki-clad men cautiously moving through the ruins to close in on the insurgent positions.

At 0930hrs both Pearse and Connolly addressed the GPO garrison and gave a version of events that saw success being achieved on all fronts and a popular rising being enacted throughout the country. It was precisely the note that Pearse had hoped to strike, but an analysis of the situation outside would have soon dispelled the rhetoric. Several thousand men were now holding the cordons north of the river and their sole task was to prevent a breakout and reduce the area occupied by the Rebels house by house, brick by brick. To emphasize this, one of the 18-pdrs was brought up to Great Britain Street from where it fired upon Arnott's drapery store, which butted onto the rear of the GPO. At the same time the guns in Westmoreland and D'Olier streets began again to engage targets along the quays and in Sackville Street over open sights.

Ruins of the GPO as seen from the top of the Nelson Pillar. The damage can be plainly seen through the windows and from the roof and upper floors of A Block, which faced onto Sackville Street. (Courtesy National Museum of Ireland, Dublin – HE1190/B273)

It was at this stage that it dawned upon the Provisional Government that the British were not intending on making the anticipated frontal assault on the GPO, and it was therefore decided to evacuate the female members of the garrison under the protection of a Red Cross flag – despite this, several women, including Connolly's secretary Winifred Carney, were to stay until the end.

As the day progressed the fires that had taken hold on the upper floors began to burn out of control, and it was soon apparent that the

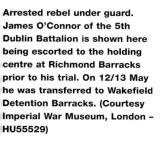

numerous fire hoses that were being played across the inferno were simply delaying the inevitable. The British may not choose to attack the building but nevertheless it was doomed, and an alternative position needed to be found.

At 1800hrs the wounded were evacuated through a tunnel that led from the rear of the GPO to the Coliseum Theatre, and, an hour later, when it looked as if the end had been reached, all prisoners that had been taken by the insurgents were brought downstairs and told to make a run for safety. Back in the GPO, the O'Rahilly had volunteered to lead a party of men to secure the site of a new headquarters in the Williams and Woods factory in Great Britain Street. As he assembled his men, he jokingly remarked 'English speakers to the front, Irish speakers to the rear'. He himself took post in advance of his men.

As the small body of men made its way up Moore Street, soldiers manning a barricade opened fire and the group scattered. The O'Rahilly was hit several times and ducked into an opening on the left side of the street. After a few minutes, he raised himself up and ran eastwards across to Sackville Lane, intending to rally his men for another attack. He never made it. The British opened fire again and this time, mortally wounded, he staggered into one of the doorways where his last act was to write a final note to his wife and family. Opposed to the Rising, when it became a reality he gave it his unswerving support and was the only senior member of the Volunteer movement to be killed in action.

Chaos now reigned, a last-ditch attempt to recall the O'Rahilly's men turned into a fiasco as many of the garrison, believing it to be a breakout attempt, milled about in the streets only to be picked off by British riflemen.

Memorial plaque to the O'Rahilly in Sackville Lane. This memorial to the O'Rahilly, the only senior Volunteer officer to be killed in action during the Rising, takes the form of his final letter to his wife and family, written as he lay mortally wounded following an attempt to storm a British barricade at the junction of Moore Street and Henry Street. (Author's collection)

Some time after 2100hrs the surviving rebels began to tunnel their way from Cogan's Greengrocers in Moore Lane through neighbouring houses towards William and Woods, but by the early hours of Saturday morning they had only reached No. 16 Moore Street, and it was here that the Provisional Government established its final headquarters.

Even as the insurgents were trying to establish a new headquarters the final nail was being driven into their coffin. Late in the evening the remaining battalions of the 176th Brigade finally reached the city, as did Brigadier Peel's artillery brigade, and – had hostilities continued past Saturday afternoon – the arrival of the 59th's batteries would have given Lowe and Maxwell the use of an additional 40 or so 18-pdr guns as well as a battery of howitzers. But in his diary, Peel states that the 'guns arrived too late in the evening to be deployed for action' and that by the time that they could be brought into action 'the rebellion had fizzled out'. A clear indication that, for the duration of the Rising, the mainstay of the British artillery deployed in Dublin were the four guns from Athlone.

Across the city it appeared that events were reaching their conclusion, but fate had one final card to play. Late on the Friday afternoon, the 2/6th South Staffordshires under Lieutenant-Colonel Henry Taylor were ordered to North King Street to complete the British cordon. Arriving in the area, Taylor received some valuable local intelligence from officers of the Sherwood Foresters who were operating in adjacent streets.

Turning the enemy's own tactics against him, Taylor ordered his men to tunnel through the houses in order to keep casualties down, but despite the arrival of one of the armoured personnel carriers and the expenditure of thousands of rounds of ammunition, by midnight they had failed to make any tangible gains whatsoever and, as a result, frustration and anger began to set in.

At about 0200hrs on the Saturday morning, a party of the 2/6th South Staffordshires forced their way into No. 172 North King Street and began to abuse the occupants, many of whom had simply taken refuge in the building. Having been searched, the women were taken down into the cellar, whilst the men were taken upstairs. Sounds of scuffling were heard and then silence.

Elsewhere, the Staffordshires were making no progress whatsoever; fighting with determination Daly's men had brought them to a standstill, so that by 0900hrs only the presence of the 2/5th South Staffs coming up through Smithfield forced the Volunteers to buckle and withdraw. Again, it was only the relentless pressure and numerical superiority of the British forces that turned the enemy positions.

# SATURDAY 29 APRIL – SURRENDER

At the Rebel headquarters, the situation was strained – Clarke, the lifelong revolutionary wanted to carry on the fight, irrespective of outcome or consequences, whilst his colleagues within the Provisional Government began to waver. The crux came when Pearse witnessed a family trying to escape their burning home under cover of a white flag being cut down by British fire.

Orders were then given for all insurgent forces to observe a ceasefire of one hour's duration whilst contact was made with the British High

Command and, at 1245hrs, Nurse Elizabeth O'Farrell was sent to meet with the officer in charge of the area. Nurse O'Farrell passed through the hands of several officers before being brought before Lowe.

The general's response was that he would not treat with the Rebels unless they agreed to surrender unconditionally, and he gave Pearse's plenipotentiary half an hour's grace before hostilities would recommence. At first the Volunteer leader demurred but Lowe made his point more forcefully and at 1430hrs Pearse, escorted by Nurse O'Farrell, met Lowe at the top of Great Britain Street, where he surrendered his sword to the British officer.

Pearse and Lowe were then driven to Parkgate where, after a terse meeting with Maxwell, he signed the instrument of surrender:

> *In order to prevent the further slaughter of Dublin citizens, and in the hope of saving the lives of our followers now surrounded and hopelessly outnumbered, the members of the Provisional Government present at Headquarters have agreed to an unconditional surrender, and the Commandants of the various districts in the City and Country will order their commands to lay down arms.*

The note was countersigned by Connolly on behalf of the Citizen Army and then taken to each of the battalions in turn. Although the final surrenders would not take place until the Sunday, the Rising was effectively over.

# THE AFTERMATH

Once the various Rebel commands had surrendered, the next question that Maxwell had to face was the question of punishment and retribution.

As far as he was concerned the ringleaders of the Rebellion and their supporters were guilty of treason during time of war and, as Ireland was under martial law at the time, they should receive the ultimate penalty – death. His problem was that such executions could not take place without at least some semblance of legal impartiality, and thus he instructed that all of the prisoners would be tried by a field general court martial (FGCM), which could be held by as few as three officers. Ironically, the FGCM was designed to try cases involving troops on active service and by virtue of their trials the insurgents were given combatant status.

In his report to London, Maxwell wrote:

> *In view of the gravity of the Rebellion and its connection with German intrigue and propaganda, and in view of the great loss of life and destruction of property resulting therefrom, the General Officer Commanding in Chief Irish Command, has found it imperative to inflict the most severe sentences on the organisers of this detestable Rising and on the commanders who took an actual part in the actual fighting that occurred.*

**Watched by an officer, British troops of the Royal Dublin Fusiliers are seen searching civilians to prevent the smuggling of contraband to Rebel prisoners being held in detention prior to sentencing. (Courtesy Imperial War Museum, London – HU73487)**

This simple cross at Kilmainham Jail marks the spot where Pearse and the majority of the leaders were executed. Unable to walk, James Connolly was carried to the opposite wall where he was shot by firing squad. (Courtesy David Murphy)

*It is hoped that these examples will be sufficient to act as a deterrent to intriguers and to bring home to them that the murder of His Majesty's subjects or other acts calculated to imperil the safety of the Realm will not be tolerated.*

The proceedings were pursued with an indecent haste that made a mockery of the court itself. When Eamonn Céannt was on trial, he was offered the opportunity to call a defence witness and named his senior officer Thomas MacDonagh, only to be told that he was indisposed and could not testify. What was not admitted was that the prospective witness had been executed that morning.

As a result of the fighting over 60,000 square yards of buildings were destroyed with an estimated cost of some 2.5 million pounds sterling. To calculate the modern value this sum should be multiplied by a factor of

Coming from the cells through the gate on the left of the picture, Connolly's guards carried him a short distance to the far wall where, strapped to a chair, he was the last of the insurgent leaders to be executed. (Courtesy David Murphy)

about 30 although this would only reflect currency fluctuations and not the increase in value.

During the Rising, it is estimated that the British forces suffered around 550 casualties whilst anything up to 2,500 civilians were either killed or injured. For their part, the Rebels are acknowledged to have incurred a little under 200, to which must be added the following who were executed at Kilmainham Jail:

Patrick Pearse, Thomas Clarke and Thomas Macdonagh – executed 3 May.
Joseph Plunkett, Edward Daly, Willie Pearse and Michael O'Hanrahan – executed 4 May.
Major John MacBride – executed 5 May.
Eamonn Céannt, Michael Mallin, Con Colbert and Seán Heuston – executed 8 May.
Seán MacDermott and James Connolly – executed 12 May.
Thomas Kent was shot in Cork on 9 May whilst Sir Roger Casement, for his involvement, was hanged in Pentonville Prison, London, on 3 August 1916.

In addition, many of the Rebels were sentenced to lengthy prison terms on the British mainland where they learned the techniques that would serve them in the Anglo-Irish War of 1919–21 and the Irish Civil War of 1922.

Finally the insurgent forces were not the only ones placed on trial. For his part in the deaths of Sheehy-Skeffington and several others, Capt. Bowen-Colthurst was found guilty of two counts of murder, but was declared to be insane. He later retired to Canada on a military pension. For the murders of the men in No. 172 North King Street, no member of the 2/6th South Staffordshires was ever charged. When an identity parade was called to offer witnesses the opportunity to identify the perpetrators, it was found that several members of the battalion had been transferred back to the British mainland.

**This plaque at Kilmainham Jail lists the names of those who were executed by the British authorities for their participation in the Rising. (Courtesy David Murphy)**

# THE BATTLEFIELD TODAY

I n the time since the Easter Rising, much of central Dublin has changed from 1916, either as a result of the rebuilding of areas razed to the ground or simply in the urban development that accompanies any modern city.

The size of the city does not preclude a solo tour of the main areas of activity during the Rising, as many of the buildings that came to

**Arbour Hill Cemetery contains the grave site of those executed for their part in the Rising. The 15 men executed by the British authorities are buried here, side by side, in a single grave. (Author's collection)**

IRISHMEN & IRISHWOMEN: In the name of God & of the dead generations from which she receives her old tradition of nationhood, Ireland, through us, summons her children to her flag and strikes for her freedom. Having organised and trained her manhood through her secret revolutionary organisation, the Irish Republican Brotherhood, and through her open military organisations, the Irish Volunteers and the Irish Citizen Army, having patiently perfected her discipline, having resolutely waited for the right moment to reveal itself, she now seizes that moment, and, supported by her exiled children in America and by gallant allies in Europe, but relying in the first on her own str

**As a backdrop to the graves of the 15 men executed by the British authorities, the text of the proclamation of the Irish Republic is reproduced both in Gaelic and English. (Author's collection)**

prominence during the events of Easter 1916 are within easy reach of the city centre and can be easily identified on most readily available tourist maps.

The GPO Building, in O'Connell Street, was rebuilt after the Rising and is now a fully functioning post office, whilst, south of the river Liffey, Dublin Castle, Trinity College, and St Stephen's Green are all within a reasonable distance of each other.

In the Western part of the city, at Kilmainham, the Royal Hospital, which was the official residence of the British commanding general in Ireland, and the jail, where the executions were carried out, are both a short bus journey from O'Connell Street.

Collins Barracks – the former Royal Barracks, and now part of the National Museum of Ireland – is served by its own LUAS stop, and adjacent to the Museum is the National Monument and Burial Site at Arbour Hill where the men executed by the British were buried in a single grave.

Northumberland Road, arguably the scene of perhaps the bitterest fighting during Easter Week, lies to the south-east of Merrion Square. Although the site of Clanwilliam House has been redeveloped, No. 25 and the Parochial Hall remain more or less as they were in 1916. The Schoolhouse, abandoned by the ambush party early during the engagement has since been rebuilt as a hotel/restaurant whilst retaining the original exterior, and is a good place to pause and reflect upon the fate of the inexperienced Sherwood Foresters as they received their baptism of fire.

As a worthwhile alternative to a solo tour, Conor Costick and Lorcan Collins, authors of the *The Easter Rising – A Guide to Dublin in 1916*, organize a guided walking tour based upon their book.

# BIBLIOGRAPHY

## Primary sources

File CO 903/19, Public Records Office, Kew
File WO 35/67, Public Records Office, Kew
File WO 35/69, Public Records Office, Kew

## Secondary sources

Barton, Brian, *From Behind A Closed Door – Secret Court Martial Records of the 1916 Easter Rising*
    Blackstaff Press: Belfast, 2002
Bradbridge, Colonel E. U. (ed.), *59th Division 1915–1918* Naval & Military Press: London,
Brennan-Whitmore, W. J., *Dublin Burning – The Easter Rising from behind the barricades* Gill &
    Macmillan: Dublin 1996
Brunicardi, Dáire, *The Sea Hound – The Story of an Irish Ship* The Collins Press: Cork, 2001
Caulfield, Max, *The Easter Rebellion – Dublin 1916* Roberts Rineheart: Boulder CO, 1995
Chappell, Mike, *Men-at-Arms 391: The British Army in World War (1) The Western Front 1914–16*
    Osprey Publishing: Oxford, 2005
Chappell, Mike, *Men-at-Arms 402: The British Army in World War 1 (2) The Western Front 1916–18*
    Osprey Publishing: Oxford, 2005
Clarke, Dale, *New Vanguard 94: British Artillery 1914–19 Field Army Artillery* Osprey Publishing:
    Oxford, 2004
Coffey, Thomas, *Agony at Easter – The 1916 Irish Uprising* Pelican: Baltimore, 1971
Coogan, Tim Pat, *1916: The Easter Rising* Orion Books: London, 2005
Coogan, Tim Pat, *De Valera – Long Fellow, Long Shadow* Arrow Books: London, 1993
Costick, Conor, and Collins, Lorcan, *The Easter Rising – A Guide to Dublin in 1916* O'Brien Press:
    Dublin, 2000
Dangerfield, George, *The Damnable Question – 120 Years of Anglo-Irish Conflict* Little, Brown & Co.:
    Boston, 1976
De Rosa, Peter, *Rebels – The Irish Rising of 1916* Ballantine Books: New York, 1992
Duff, Charles, *Six Days to Shake an Empire* Curtis Books: New York, 1966
Fergusson, Sir James, *The Curragh Incident* Faber & Faber: London 1964
FitzGerald, Desmond, *Desmond's Rising – Memoirs 1913 to Easter 1916* Liberties Press: Dublin, 2006
Foy, Michael, and Barton, Brian, *The Easter Rising* Sutton Publishing: Stroud, 2004
James, Brigadier E. A., *British Regiments, 1914–1918* Naval & Military Press: London, 1993
Kenny, Michael *The Road to Freedom – Photographs and Memorabilia from the 1916 Rising and
    afterwards* Country House Press/National Museum of Ireland: Dublin, 2001
McHugh, Roger (ed.), *Dublin 1916* Desmond Elliott: New York, 1976
Martin, F. X. (ed.), *The Irish Volunteers 1913–1915* James Duffy and Co.: Dublin, 1963
Nowlan, Kevin (ed.), *The Making of 1916 – Studies in the History of the Rising* Stationary Office:
    Dublin, 1969
O'Malley, Ernie, *Army Without Banners*\* New English Library: London, 1967
\*Originally entitled *On Another Man's Wound*, published 1937.
O'Rahilly, Aodogán, *Winding the Clock – The O'Rahilly and the 1916 Rising* Lilliput Press: Dublin, 1991
Purdon, Edward, *The 1916 Rising* Mercier Press: Cork, 1999
Ryan, Annie, *Witnesses: Inside the Easter Rising* Liberties Press: Dublin, 2005
Stephens, James, *The Insurrection in Dublin – An eyewitness account of the Easter Rising, 1916*
    Barnes & Noble: New York, 1992.
Stewart, A. T. Q., *The Ulster Crisis* Faber & Faber: London, 1967
Townsend, Charles, *Easter 1916, The Irish Rebellion* Allen Lane: London, 2005
Trimble, David, *The Easter Rebellion of 1916* Ulster Society (Publications) Ltd: Lurgan, 1992
Warwick-Haller, Adrian & Sally (eds.), Letters from Dublin, *Easter 1916 – Alfred Fannin's Diary of the
    Rising* Irish Academic Press: Dublin, 1995
Westlake, Ray, *Men-at-Arms 245: British Territorial Units 1914–18* Osprey Publishing: Oxford, 2003
White, Gerry, and O'Shea, Brendan, *Warrior 80: Irish Volunteer Soldier 1913–23* Osprey Publishing Ltd:
    Oxford, 2003

# INDEX